LOTUS 1-2-3®

A Visual Approach for
the Beginner

Welcome to **Quick & Easy.** Designed for the true novice, this new series covers basic tasks in a simple, learn-by-doing fashion. If that sounds like old news to you, take a closer look.

Quick & Easy books are a bit like picture books. They're for people who would rather see and do than read and ponder. The books are colorful. They're full of illustrations, and accompanying text that is straightforward, concise, and easy to read.

But don't waste your time reading about our **Quick & Easy** books; start learning your new software package instead. This **Quick & Easy** book is just the place to start.

Lotus 1-2-3®
Quick & Easy

Jeff Woodward

SYBEX®

San Francisco ● Paris ● Düsseldorf ● Soest

Acquisitions Editor: David Clark
Series Editor: Christian T. S. Crumlish
Editor: Janna Hecker Clark
Technical Editor: Rebecca Moore Lyles
Word Processors: Ann Dunn, Chris Meredith
Book Designer: Helen Bruno
Chapter Art: Alissa Feinberg
Screen Graphics: Cuong Le
Page Layout and Typesetting: Len Gilbert
Proofreader/Production Assistant: Janet MacEachern
Indexer: Ted Laux
Cover Designer: Archer Design
Cover Illustrator: Richard Miller

Screen reproductions produced with HotShot Graphics.

SYBEX is a registered trademark of SYBEX Inc.

TRADEMARKS: SYBEX has attempted throughout this book to distinguish proprietary trademarks from descriptive terms by following the capitalization style used by the manufacturer.

SYBEX is not affiliated with any manufacturer.

Every effort has been made to supply complete and accurate information. However, SYBEX assumes no responsibility for its use, nor for any infringement of the intellectual property rights of third parties which would result from such use.

Library of Congress Card Number: 92-61253
ISBN: 0-89588-867-X

Manufactured in the United States of America
10 9 8 7 6 5 4 3 2 1

ACKNOWLEDGMENTS

●

Lotus 1-2-3 Quick & Easy presents a new and unique concept in computer book tutorials. The book would not exist were it not for a great deal of hard work by many talented individuals at SYBEX. I would like to thank everyone for their perseverance, patience, and craftsmanship. I would also like to thank the following individuals:

Christian Crumlish, my developmental editor, who has supported my ideas and work through yet another book. He was always there when I needed assistance.

Janna Clark, my copy editor, for her consistently kind and gentle guidance in the organization and detail of this book. She was never far from my thoughts.

Delia Brown, for all the help she gave me to conquer the screen graphic difficulties associated with this new, four-color concept.

It is a pleasure to once again to thank Dianne King and Dave Clark, Acquisition Editors; Barbara Gordon, Managing Editor; and Dr. Rudolph Langer, Editor-in-Chief, for their continuing confidence in and support of my work.

Congratulations and thanks go to the Lotus Development Corporation for creating such a sensational program. May they continue to have great success in the future.

Jeff Woodward
9 August 1992
Valencia, California

Contents
at a Glance

●

Contents

Welcome to *Lotus 1-2-3 Quick & Easy*, a visual, step-by-step guide to the powerful tools available in Lotus 1-2-3 Release 2.4. If you are new to computerized number crunching, are familiar with other versions of 1-2-3, or would like to make the transition from another spreadsheet program to 1-2-3, then this book is an excellent place to begin.

The unique visual approach of this book enables it to reflect as closely as possible the actual experience of using 1-2-3 at the computer. *Lotus 1-2-3 Quick & Easy* is an efficient and effective tool for those who want to learn how to create spreadsheets as they work at the computer, but don't really want to read pages and pages of text to accomplish their goal. The exercises are not lengthy, providing the most benefit in the least amount of time.

Why, you ask, is this book any better than the documentation that came with my 1-2-3 program? The 1-2-3 documentation, excellent as it is, is primarily a reference manual listing of the many functions of the program. You are not always shown how to use the information. *Lotus 1-2-3 Quick & Easy* is a carefully designed tutorial that builds upon the increases your level of skill and confidence in a logical, sequential manner. You are directly involved from the first moment, activating keystroke commands or using a mouse to create sample worksheets step by step. With the visual format, clear, concisely written instructions are followed by an illustration of what should appear on your monitor. Descriptive screen labels and notes provide some tips and shortcuts for using many of the powerful options available with 1-2-3. You will be surprised at how quick and easy it is to get up and running with 1-2-3 Release 2.4.

What Makes it Quick and Easy?

Unlike most computer books *Lotus 1-2-3 Quick & Easy* uses a balanced mix of text and screen illustrations in a series of practical lessons

designed to let you teach yourself to use the program. Each section of
the book is broken up into lessons that present graphic and written instructions, with most instructions followed by an illustration of what
you should actually see on your computer screen.

Here is an example of the kind of steps you will follow in the lessons in
this book:

1. Turn your computer on and select /Print ➤ Printer ➤
Range.

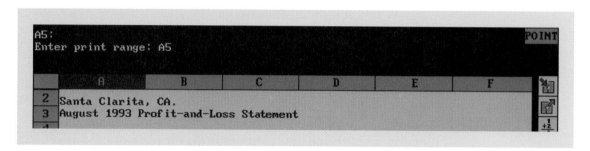

2. Press **F3** (the Name key).

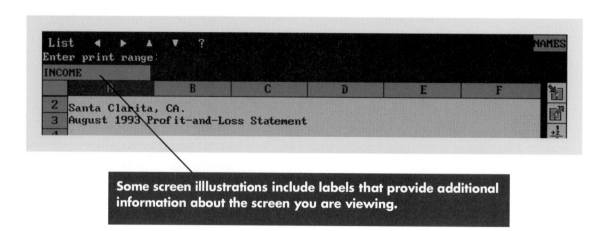

**Some screen illlustrations include labels that provide additional
information about the screen you are viewing.**

Step 1   You are first instructed to turn your printer on. Then, you select the specified menu items using the keyboard or the mouse. When you complete the instruction, your screen should look like the one shown below the step 1 instructions.

Step 2   Press the **F3** function key, which Lotus calls the Name key. When you complete the instruction, your screen should look like the one shown below the step 2 instruction.

You will also see notes like this one throughout the book:

 Notes Provide Supplementary Information—This special feature supplies helpful hints, warnings and additional information to assist you in the learning process.

When you see two connected keys, such as **Alt-F4**, you should press and hold down the first key (the **Alt** key in this case), press the second key (the **F4** key here), and then release both keys.

Before You Begin

Many people become intimidated when they have to read instructions of any sort. I want to give you some quick advice about intimidation to those of you who are new to computers: Forget it! This book is designed to make getting started with 1- 2-3 as easy and as painless as possible.

So relax and begin at the beginning. By the time you complete the first two parts you will have created your first worksheet, printed it, and saved it for future editing. I think you will be surprised by how easy it is.

PART ONE

Getting Started with 1-2-3

This is the place to begin if you are new to Lotus 1-2-3. Lessons in this part will teach you how to start and quit the program, move around in the worksheet, and create and save a worksheet. There are many types of documents that you can construct using 1-2-3, but we'll confine our discussion to a simple profit-and-loss statement to make learning easier.

- Starting 1-2-3

- Using SmartIcons

- Quitting 1-2-3

- Entering Numerical Values, Formulas, and Functions

- Saving Your Worksheet

Starting and Quitting 1-2-3

To begin, let's start with the basics. This lesson will show you how simple it is to get in and out of the program.

Starting 1-2-3

You can start 1-2-3 at the DOS prompt by simply typing **123** and pressing ↵. The 1-2-3 program will start and the worksheet screen will be displayed. If you prefer, you can also start the program from the Lotus Access System:

1. At the DOS prompt, type **CD\123R24** and press ↵ to change to the 1-2-3 directory.

2. Type **LOTUS** and press ↵. The Access System screen appears.

```
 Create worksheets, graphs, and databases
 1-2-3        PrintGraph      Translate      Install      Exit


                              Lotus
                        1-2-3 Access Menu
                          Release 2.4

             Copyright 1990, 1991, 1992 Lotus Development Corporation
                          All Rights Reserved.


 To select a program to start, do one of the following:

    *  Use  ←, →, HOME, or END to move the menu pointer
       to the program you want and then press ENTER.

    *  Type the first character of the program's name.

 Press F1 (HELP) for more information.
```

Executes the 1-2-3 program

Transfers data between 1-2-3 and other programs

Returns you to DOS

A special program used to print graphics

Installs the 1-2-3 program and changes hardware settings

3. Press ↵. The 1-2-3 worksheet appears.

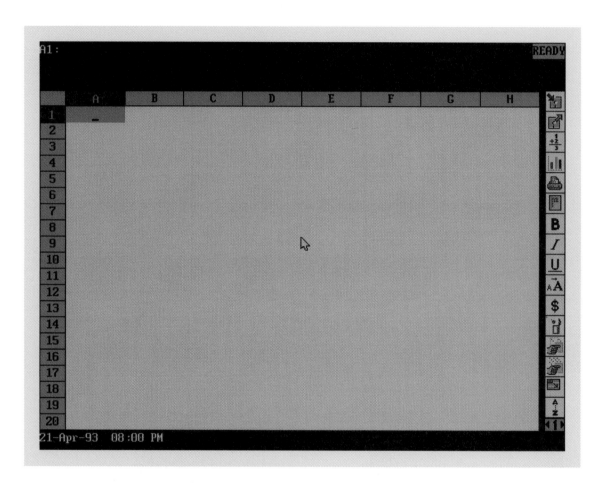

Quitting 1-2-3

To exit 1-2-3, you must select the Quit option from the main menu.

1. Press / or move the mouse pointer into the control panel (the top of the screen) to display the main menu.

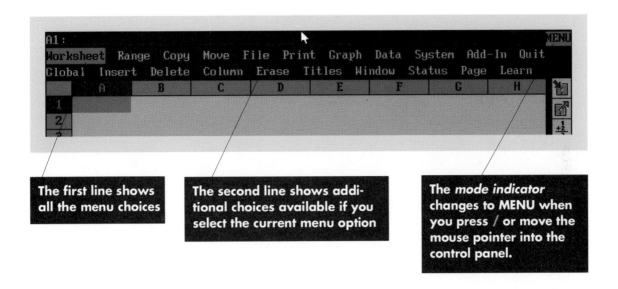

The first line shows all the menu choices

The second line shows additional choices available if you select the current menu option

The *mode indicator* changes to MENU when you press / or move the mouse pointer into the control panel.

2. Press ← once to move the highlight to Quit and press ↵, or place the mouse pointer on Quit and click the left mouse button.

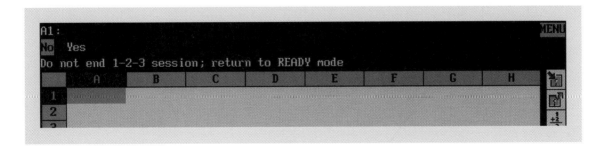

3. Move the highlight to Yes and press ↵, or click on Yes
with the mouse. If you started 1-2-3 directly from the DOS
prompt, you will return to the DOS prompt. Otherwise,
you will return to the Access System menu.

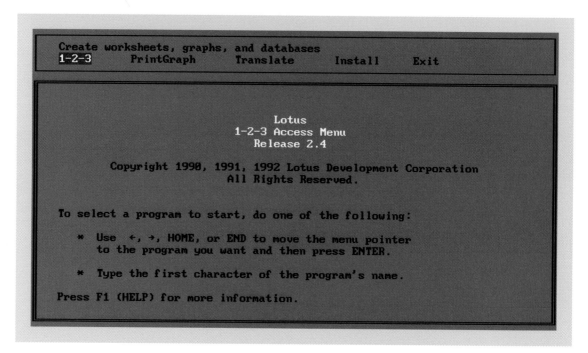

4. Click on Exit, or move the highlight to Exit and press ↵ to
leave the 1-2-3 Access System.

2 Finding Your Way around the Worksheet

The 1-2-3 worksheet has four distinct areas: the *worksheet area*, the *control panel*, the *status line*, and the *SmartIcons*. Let's start 1-2-3 and take a brief look at each area.

 ● Note Lesson 1 contains an explanation of how to start 1-2-3. If you need a reminder, go back to Lesson 1 before continuing.

The Worksheet Area

The worksheet area is where you display and calculate your worksheet entries. It is constructed of rows and columns.

The following illustration gives you the names of some of the most important elements of the 1-2-3 screen.

Don't worry about memorizing all these names and explanations. As soon as you start using 1-2-3 you'll get a hands-on feel for these elements.

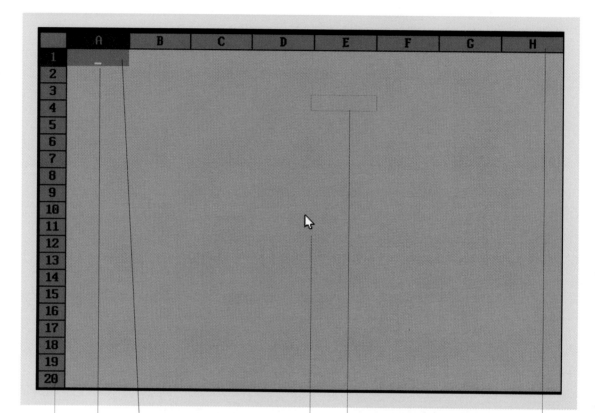

This is the *cell pointer*. It highlights the cell you are currently working with. You can move the pointer to any cell in the worksheet.

This is the *cursor*. It marks the location where characters are entered or deleted.

These numbers indicate the *rows* in which you can place data. Rows are numbered from 1 to 8,192. This screen displays only 20 rows at a time.

These letters indicate the *columns* in which you can place data. There are 256 columns, lettered A–Z, AA–AZ, BA–BZ, and so on to IV. This screen shows only eight columns, but you can change the screen width to show more.

This is a *cell*. It is formed by the intersection of a column and a row. This cell is called E5 because it is the location where column E and row 5 meet.

This is the *mouse pointer*. By moving your mouse, you can use the pointer to highlight a cell, select menu and SmartIcon options, and perform several 1-2-3 tasks.

The Control Panel

The control panel is where you enter and edit data to be displayed on the worksheet, enter the formulas you want 1-2-3 to execute, and select commands to activate 1-2-3's many powerful features.

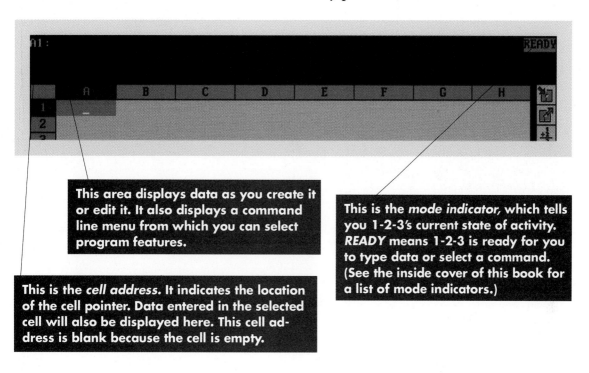

This area displays data as you create it or edit it. It also displays a command line menu from which you can select program features.

This is the *mode indicator,* which tells you 1-2-3's current state of activity. *READY* means 1-2-3 is ready for you to type data or select a command. (See the inside cover of this book for a list of mode indicators.)

This is the *cell address.* It indicates the location of the cell pointer. Data entered in the selected cell will also be displayed here. This cell address is blank because the cell is empty.

The Status Line

The status line displays information about the current work session.

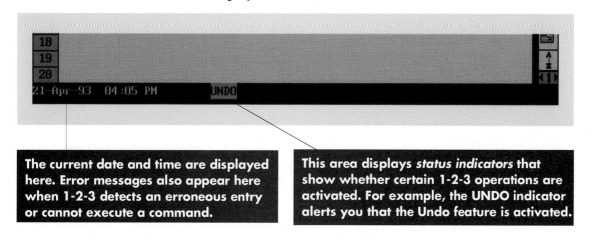

The current date and time are displayed here. Error messages also appear here when 1-2-3 detects an erroneous entry or cannot execute a command.

This area displays *status indicators* that show whether certain 1-2-3 operations are activated. For example, the UNDO indicator alerts you that the Undo feature is activated.

SmartIcons and Palettes

SmartIcons speed up the execution of 1-2-3 options and macros. Instead of selecting an option from the menu system, you can use a mouse or the keyboard to select the corresponding SmartIcon.

The number of SmartIcon palettes available is determined by the type of monitor you have and whether Wysiwyg is attached. (Wysiwyg is automatically attached when you start 1-2-3.) With a VGA monitor and Wysiwyg attached, seven palettes are available.

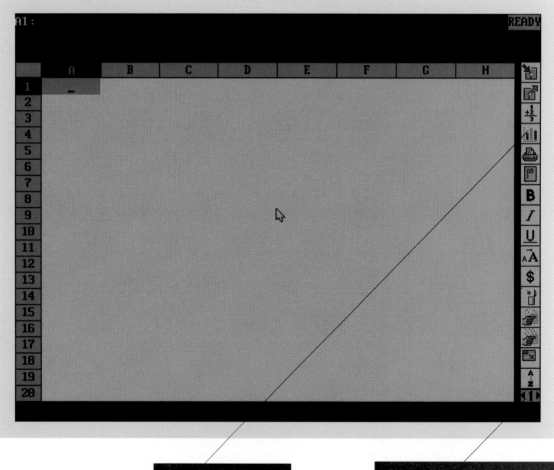

SmartIcon palette

The current palette number

Moving the Cell Pointer

In order to place data in the many cells that make up the worksheet, you must be able to move the cell pointer to the desired locations. There are several ways to move the cell pointer, using both the keyboard and the mouse. Here, we will cover the basic cell pointer movements for both. Your screen should still display a blank worksheet with the cell pointer located in cell A1.

1. Press → ten times to move the cell pointer to cell K1. Notice that columns A–C disappear off the left side of the worksheet.

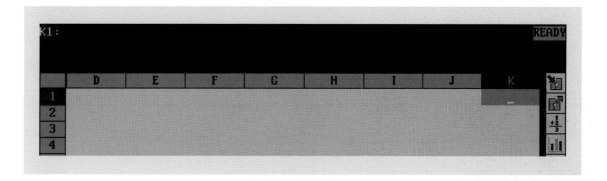

● Note The Num Lock Key—If you use the arrow keys that are on the numeric keypad, be sure Num Lock is off. (When Num Lock is on, you will see *NUM* highlighted on the status line in the bottom right corner of your screen.) If Num Lock is on, numbers will appear on your screen and the cell pointer will not move. Delete the numbers by pressing **Backspace**, then press **Num Lock** to turn this feature off.

2. Press ↓ 24 times to move the cell pointer to cell K25. Notice that rows 1–5 disappear off the top of the worksheet.

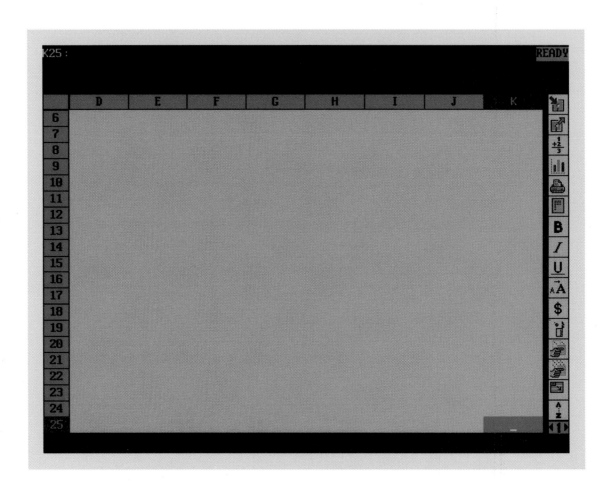

3. Place the mouse pointer in cell F25 and click the left mouse button to move the cell pointer to cell F25.

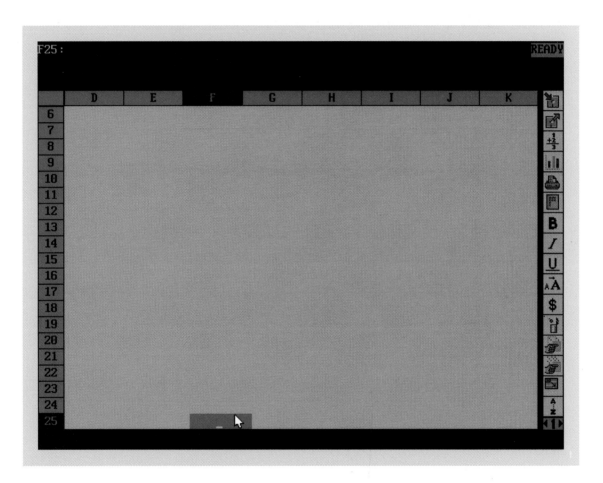

4. Place the mouse pointer in cell F10 and click to move the cell pointer to cell F10.

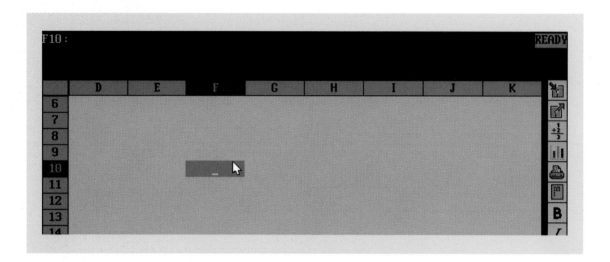

5. Press **Home** to return the cell pointer to cell A1. (You can do this from anywhere on the worksheet.)

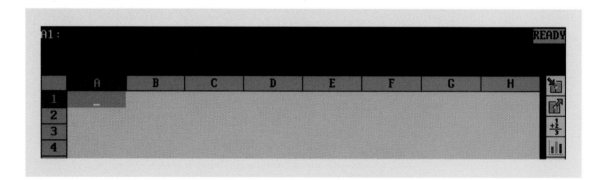

6. Press **End** → to move the cell pointer to cell IV1. Column IV is the 256th and last column on the worksheet.

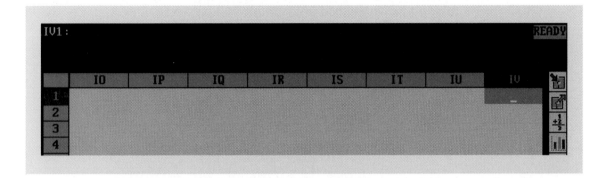

7. Press **End** ↓ to move the cell pointer to cell IV8192. Row 8192 is the last row of the worksheet.

● Note Cursor Key Limitations—Pressing **End** and any arrow key will move the cell pointer in the direction of the arrow to the nearest cell containing data, to the farthest cell containing data if this movement is made across consecutive data-containing cells, or to the farthest blank cell if no data is encountered.

8. Press **Home** to return to cell A1.

9. Press **PageDown** to move the cell pointer one full screen (20 rows) to cell A21.

10. Press **PageUp** to move the cell pointer one full screen to cell A1.

11. Press **F5**. This is the Go To key, which allows you to type in a specific cell address and move the cell pointer to that location.

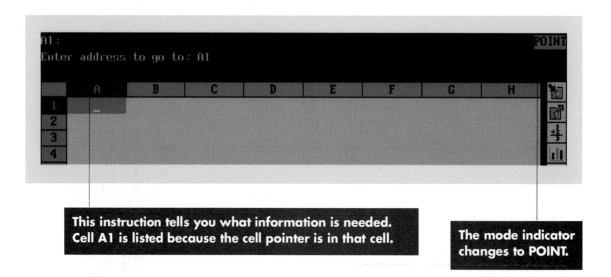

This instruction tells you what information is needed. Cell A1 is listed because the cell pointer is in that cell.

The mode indicator changes to POINT.

12. Type **G13** and then press ⏎, or move the mouse pointer to the control panel and click the left mouse button to move the cell pointer to cell G13.

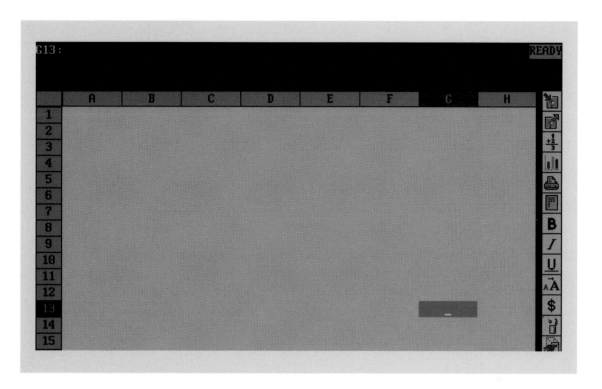

13. Press **Home** to return the cell pointer to cell A1.

Using SmartIcons

3

In this lesson we'll learn how to execute a SmartIcon, using both the mouse and keyboard. You will also learn how to add and remove icons from a palette.

Executing SmartIcons

To execute a SmartIcon, place the mouse pointer on the icon and click the left mouse button. If the icon you want to activate is not displayed on the current palette, you will have to change palettes. Place the mouse pointer on the right arrow next to the palette number and click the left mouse button to move forward through the seven icon palettes. To move backward, click on the left arrow next to the palette number.

To execute an icon using the keyboard, first press Alt-F7 to highlight the topmost icon. Then, press ↑ or ↓ to move to the icon you want, and press ↵ to execute it. (You can press Home or End to quickly move to the top or bottom of the icon palette.) You can change palettes with the keyboard by pressing Alt-F7 and ← or →.

Customizing a SmartIcon Palette

Palette 1 can be modified by adding, removing, or moving icons. This enables you to customize the palette for your most frequently performed tasks.

Adding an Icon

Let's add an icon to Palette 1. Remember, to change palettes, use the palette-number icon in the lower-right corner of your screen.

1. Press **Alt-F7** and ← twice, or click twice on the left arrow of the palette-number icon, or to display Palette 6.

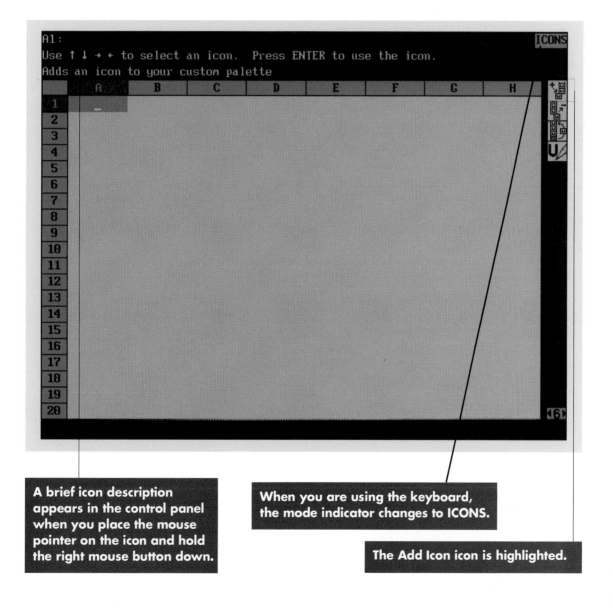

A brief icon description appears in the control panel when you place the mouse pointer on the icon and hold the right mouse button down.

When you are using the keyboard, the mode indicator changes to ICONS.

The Add Icon icon is highlighted.

2. Press ↵, or click on the Add Icon icon

to display the Custom Palette instruction box.

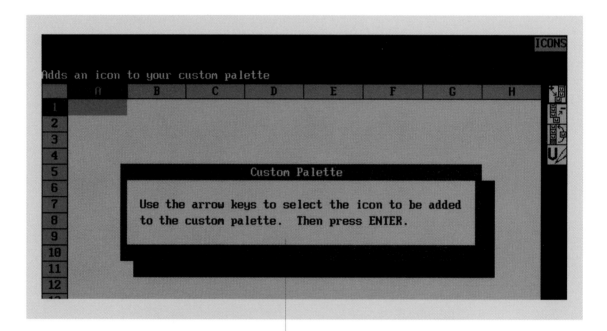

The Custom Palette box provides instructions for selecting an icon with the keyboard or the mouse, depending on which method you use.

3. Press ← twice, or click on the left palette-number arrow twice to display Palette 4.

4. Press ↑ or ↓ to highlight the Undo icon

and press ↵, or click on the Undo icon to add it to Palette 1.

5. Display Palette 1. Notice the Undo icon appears at the bottom of the palette.

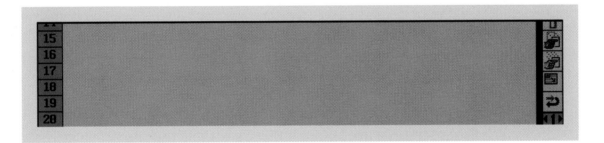

 ● Note Icon Replacement—A full SmartIcon palette contains 16 icons. When you add a new icon to a full palette, the sixteenth icon is replaced by the new icon. In the exercise above, the Undo icon replaced the Sort A To Z icon.

Removing an Icon

Let's remove an icon from Palette 1.

The procedure is very similar to the one you just learned for adding an icon.

1. Display SmartIcon Palette 6.

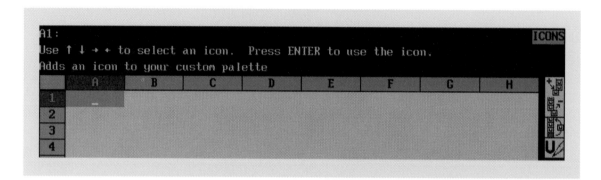

2. Select the Delete Icon icon.

The Custom Palette instructions box appears along with Palette 1.

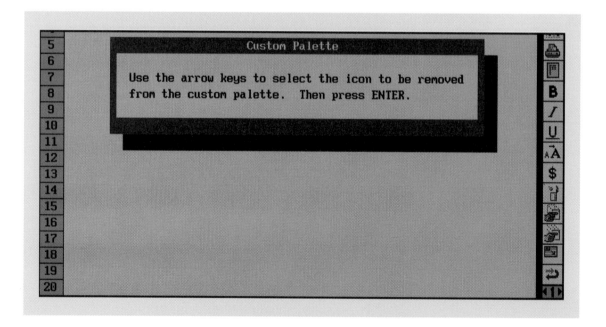

3. Select the Undo icon. Then, display Palette 1. The Undo icon is gone from the palette.

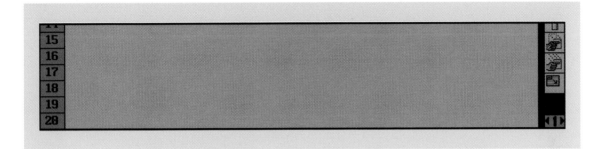

4. Follow steps 1–5 in the section "Adding an Icon" and add the Sort Database A To Z icon

(found on Palette 3) back onto Palette 1.

Moving an Icon

You can move an icon on Palette 1 from one location to another. Let's try it.

1. Display Palette 6.

2. Select the Move icon.

The Custom Palette instructions box appears along with Palette 1.

3. Select the Retrieve File icon

and read the instructions in the Custom Palette box.

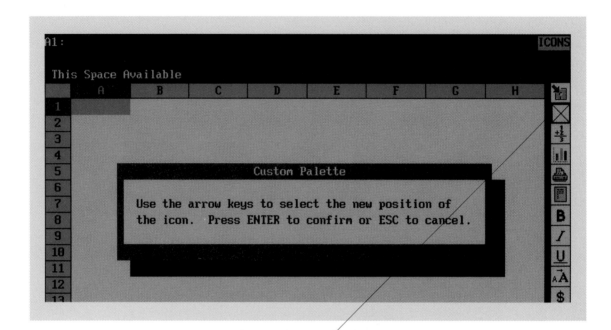

The icon to be moved becomes an X.

4. Press ↓ to move the highlight to the Print Icon

or click the mouse pointer on the Print Icon. You are returned to Palette 6.

5. Display Palette 1 to see the Retrieve File icon in its new location.

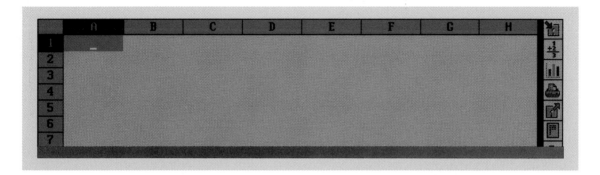

6. Follow steps 1–5 above and move the Retrieve File icon back to it's former location (second from the top).

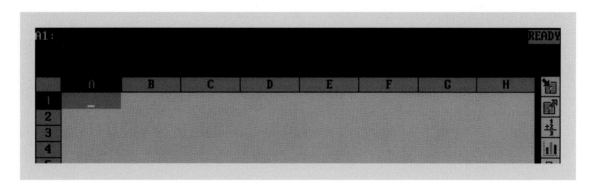

In Lesson 4, you will begin to create your first 1-2-3 document.

Labeling Your Worksheet

4

The columns and rows of numbers that make up a spreadsheet have no meaning unless you give them names that describe what the numbers represent. 1-2-3 calls these names *labels*. You can place any kind of label on a worksheet: years, months, days, dates, subject titles, budget items, and so on.

In this lesson, we will create a worksheet with labels that title the spreadsheet, specify time periods, and identify several income and expense items.

Entering Labels

1. With the cell pointer in cell A1, type **BRIARCLIFF AVIATION**. (As on a typewriter keyboard, pressing **Caps Lock** will allow you to type all capital letters.) Use **Backspace** to correct any typos.

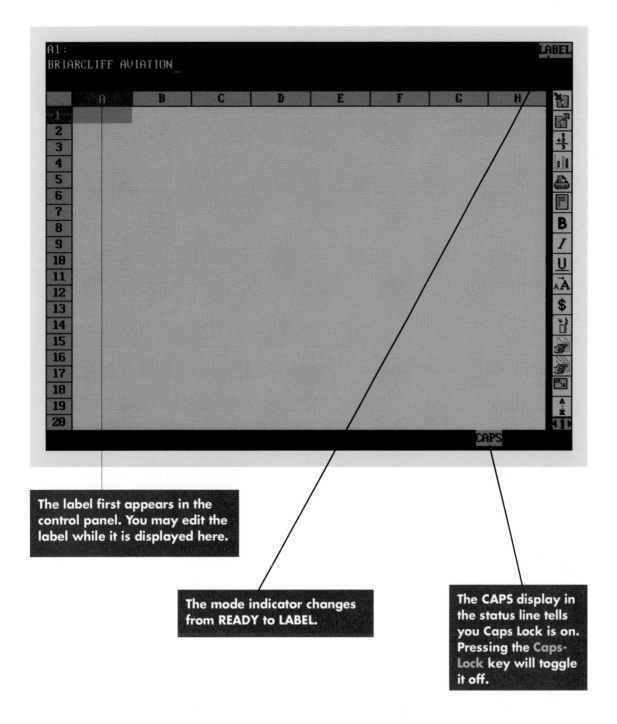

The label first appears in the control panel. You may edit the label while it is displayed here.

The mode indicator changes from **READY** to **LABEL**.

The CAPS display in the status line tells you Caps Lock is on. Pressing the Caps-Lock key will toggle it off.

2. Press ↵ to place the label on the worksheet in cell A1. The cell pointer remains in cell A1.

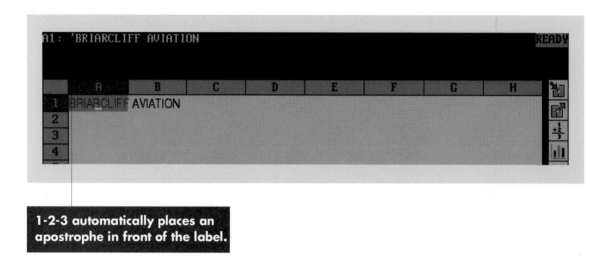

1-2-3 automatically places an apostrophe in front of the label.

3. Click on cell A2 or press ↓ once. Press **Caps Lock** to turn this feature off, type **Santa Clarita, CA.**, and press ↵.

4. Move the cell pointer to cell A3. Type **August 1993 Profit-and-Loss Statement** and press ↵.

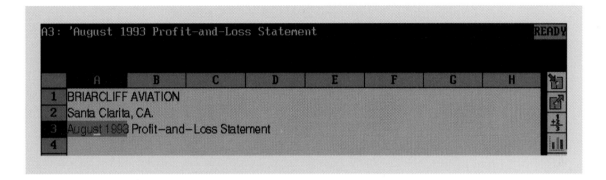

5. Move the cell pointer to cell C5.

6. Type **^Week 1** and press →. The cell pointer moves to cell D5 and the label is placed in cell C5.

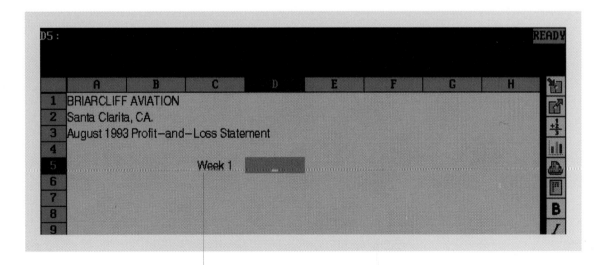

The caret (^) centers the label in cell C5.

> ● **Note** Label Prefixes—Label prefixes allow you to position a label within a cell. You may type the prefix as you type the label, or you may edit the prefix anytime after it's placed on the worksheet. An apostrophe (') aligns the label with the left edge of the cell, a caret (^) centers the label within the cell, quotation marks (") align the label with the right edge of the cell, and a backslash (\) repeats the label across the width of the cell. Text labels entered without prefixes are automatically aligned with the left edge of the cell. If the label begins with a number or symbol, however, you *must* type a label prefix in front of the label or 1-2-3 will beep and not accept the entry.

7. Type ^Week 2 and press →. Do the same for Week 3 and Week 4. All the column labels are now entered on the worksheet.

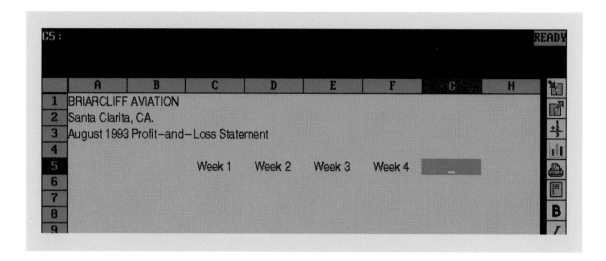

8. Move the pointer to cell C6, type *, and press →. (If you mistakenly press /, you will see the main menu in the control panel. Press **Esc** to get rid of the menu and try again.)

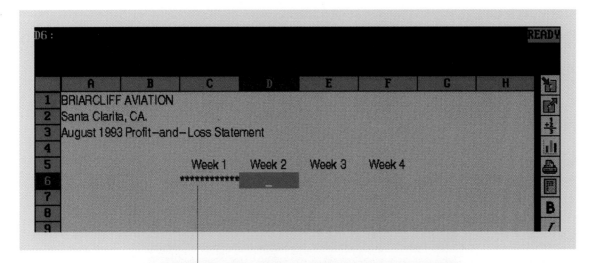

The * is repeated across the full width of cell C6.

9. Repeat step 8 three times to place asterisks across cells D6 through F6.

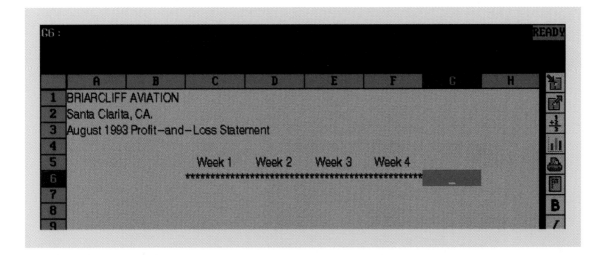

10. Move the pointer to cell A7. Type **INCOME** and press ↓.

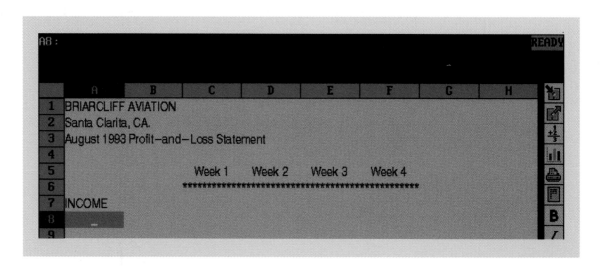

● Note Long Labels—A long label is one containing more characters than will fit in a single cell. If the cells to the right of the label are empty of data, the label will run over into those cells. If data exists in the adjacent cells, however, the label will be cut off at the left edge of the first cell containing data.

11. Type in the remaining labels as shown below. Double-check to make sure you type the correct label in the correct cell. Remember, after you type a label, press ↓ or use the mouse to place the label in the cell and move the pointer to the next cell.

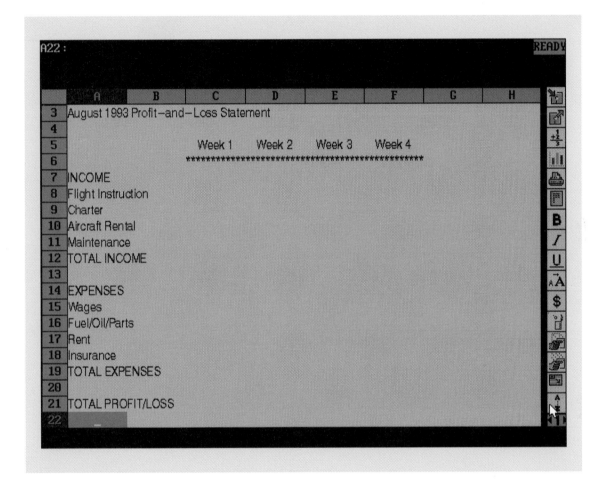

Entering Numerical Values

5

Now you are ready to place numerical data into the appropriate cells of the worksheet. Let's enter the raw income and expense data first. Then, in the next lesson, "Using Formulas," we'll apply the formulas necessary to analyze the raw data.

Placing Data in the Cells

1. Move the cell pointer to cell C8 and type **1600**. Do not press ↵ or any arrow key yet.

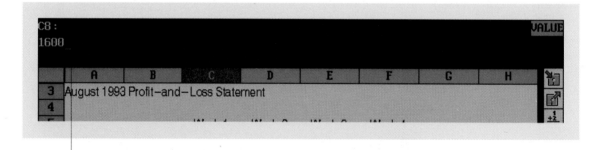

As you type a value, it is displayed on the control panel. Edit it, if necessary, *before* you place it on the worksheet.

● **Note** Guidelines for Entering Values—Begin entries with a number or numerical symbol such as + – @ . (# $. Do not include commas or spaces in an entry, or type more than one decimal point in any single entry. Dollar signs are not normally displayed on the worksheet—see Part Two: "Editing Your Worksheet" for instructions on how to display dollar signs and commas in numerical entries.

2. When the value displayed in the control panel is correct, press →. The value is placed in C8 and the cell pointer moves to D8.

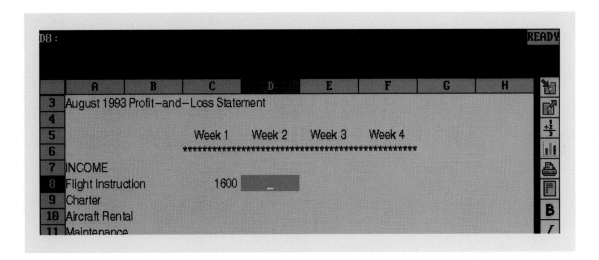

• Note As with entering labels in the last lesson, you do not have to press ⏎ to enter a numerical value, as long as you press → or another arrow key when you are done.

3. Type 1200 and press →.

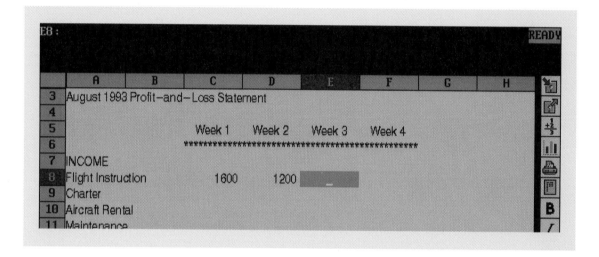

4. Using this same procedure, enter the values shown below. (If you enter an incorrect value, don't try to change it now. We'll learn how to do this later.)

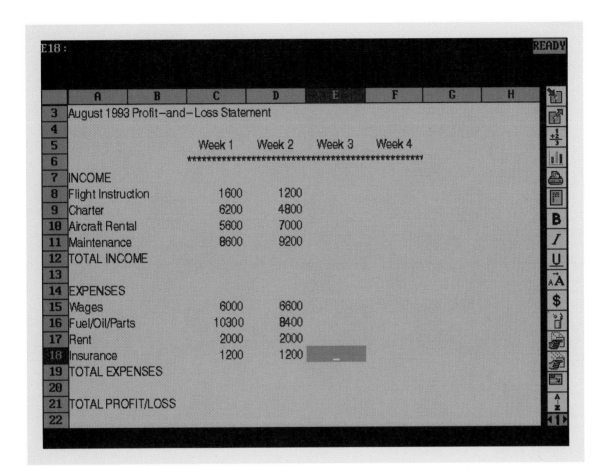

Using Formulas

Now that you've entered your income and expense figures, it's time to make sense of your data. To do that, you can use formulas.

Formulas can be as simple or as complex as necessary. 1-2-3 can perform many mathematical computations, from simple addition to trigonometric functions. In this lesson, we'll explore the more basic mathematical formulas you will deal with on a day-to-day basis.

Let's compute the total income, expense, and profit/loss figures for the worksheet you've just created.

Entering Formulas

1. Move the cell pointer to cell C12.

	Week 1	Week 2	Week 3	Week 4
5				
6	**			
7 INCOME				
8 Flight Instruction	1600	1200		
9 Charter	6200	4800		
10 Aircraft Rental	5600	7000		
11 Maintenance	8600	9200		
12 TOTAL INCOME				
13				
14 EXPENSES				
15 Wages	6000	6600		
16 Fuel/Oil/Parts	10300	8400		

2. Type **+C8+C9+C10+C11.** This formula will tell 1-2-3 to add together the values stored in these four cells.

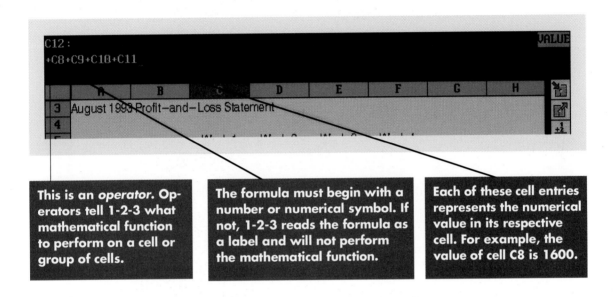

This is an *operator*. Operators tell 1-2-3 what mathematical function to perform on a cell or group of cells.

The formula must begin with a number or numerical symbol. If not, 1-2-3 reads the formula as a label and will not perform the mathematical function.

Each of these cell entries represents the numerical value in its respective cell. For example, the value of cell C8 is 1600.

● Note Some Common Operators—The plus sign (+) denotes addition or a positive number and a minus sign (–) indicates subtraction or a negative number. An asterisk (*) shows multiplication, a slash (/) denotes division, and a caret (^) indicates exponentiation. The < sign is the less-than operator, while the > sign is the greater-than operator.

3. Press → to place the formula in cell C12. The total income appears in cell C12.

		Week 1	Week 2	Week 3	Week 4
5					
6		**			
7	INCOME				
8	Flight Instruction	1600	1200		
9	Charter	6200	4800		
10	Aircraft Rental	5600	7000		
11	Maintenance	8600	9200		
12	TOTAL INCOME	22000			
13					
14	EXPENSES				
15	Wages	6000	6600		
16	Fuel/Oil/Parts	10300	8400		

4. Type **+D8+D9+D10+D11** and press →. The total income for the Week 2 column now appears in cell D12.

		Week 1	Week 2	Week 3	Week 4
5					
6		**			
7	INCOME				
8	Flight Instruction	1600	1200		
9	Charter	6200	4800		
10	Aircraft Rental	5600	7000		
11	Maintenance	8600	9200		
12	TOTAL INCOME	22000	22200		
13					
14	EXPENSES				
15	Wages	6000	6600		
16	Fuel/Oil/Parts	10300	8400		

5. Move the cell pointer to cell C21. Type **+C12–C19** and press →.

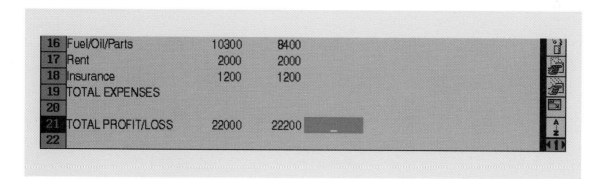

16	Fuel/Oil/Parts	10300	8400
17	Rent	2000	2000
18	Insurance	1200	1200
19	TOTAL EXPENSES		
20			
21	TOTAL PROFIT/LOSS	22000	
22			

The TOTAL PROFIT/LOSS figure reflects only total income (C12) because we have not yet computed our total expenses (C19).

6. Type **+D12–D19** and press →. This computes the total profit/loss for Week 2.

16	Fuel/Oil/Parts	10300	8400
17	Rent	2000	2000
18	Insurance	1200	1200
19	TOTAL EXPENSES		
20			
21	TOTAL PROFIT/LOSS	22000	22200
22			

Understanding the Order of Precedence

Order of precedence refers to the order in which 1-2-3 performs mathematical calculations. Instead of calculating a formula from left to right,

1-2-3 applies algebraic rules of computation and works with operators in the following order:

> ^ (exponentiation)
>
> + *or* − (for positive or negative values)
>
> * *or* / (multiplication or division)
>
> + *or* − (for addition or subtraction)
>
> < *or* > *or* = (less-than, greater-than, or equal-to)

Operators that have the same order of precedence are executed from left to right as written. For the order of precedence for more advanced operators, consult your 1-2-3 documentation.

Overriding the Order of Precedence

You may override the order of precedence by enclosing parts of a formula in parentheses. 1-2-3 always executes operations within parentheses first.

For example, multiplication normally occurs before addition. In the formula

    C5*(A1+A2+A3)

however, the addition takes place before the multiplication. The values in cells A1 through A3 are added first because they are enclosed in parentheses. The result of this addition is then multiplied by C5. Without the parentheses, C5 would first be multiplied by A1, then that result would be added to A2, which would then be added to A3.

If you want to take a break at this point, go to Lesson 8, "Saving Your Worksheet." Otherwise, keep this worksheet on your screen and proceed to the next lesson.

7 Using Functions to Streamline Your Calculations

T yping formulas can be a cumbersome process when your worksheet has many rows and columns of figures. (Imagine having to type each cell address for ten columns containing 20 rows of numbers!) Fortunately, 1-2-3 provides functions that streamline the operation of your formulas.

Functions are abbreviated formulas that perform a specific operation on a set of values. They consist of the @ symbol and a single word that identifies the function. This lesson introduces you to 1-2-3 operations using the @SUM function. @SUM tells 1-2-3 to add together a designated group, or *range*, of cell values.

Creating Formulas with @Sum

With your worksheet on screen (see Lesson 10 if you need information on how to retrieve your file), follow these steps:

1. Move the cell pointer to cell C19. Type @SUM(.

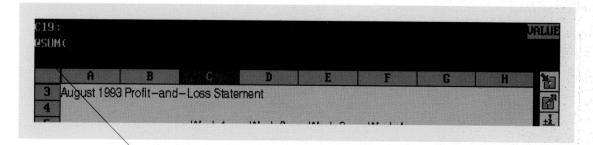

1-2-3 recognizes the @ symbol as a numerical value.

2. Move the cell pointer to cell C15.

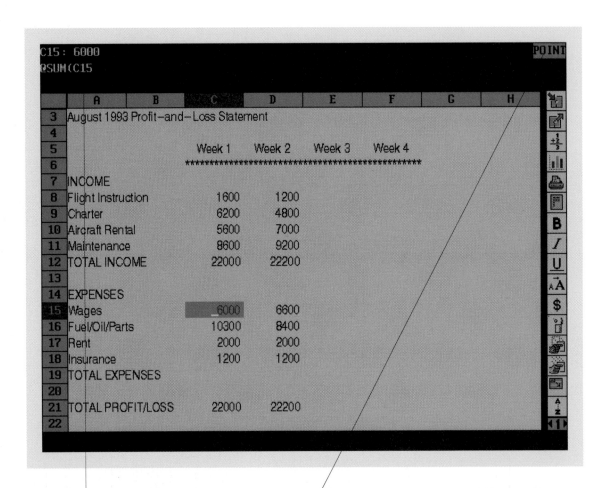

C15 is placed in the formula.

The mode indicator tells you that you are pointing at a specific cell address.

3. Press **Period**. This anchors cell C15 into the formula.

```
C15: 6000                                                    POINT
@SUM(C15..C15
```

	A	B	C	D	E	F	G	H
3	August 1993 Profit-and-Loss Statement							
4								

The two C15 entries indicate that only one cell has been pointed to so far.

4. Press ↓ to move the cell pointer to cell C18 (*do not use the mouse*).

Watch as you move the cell pointer. The range you are indicating will be highlighted and the highlight will extend with each press of ↓. Also, the second cell referred to in the formula will also change with each press, until you reach C18.

```
C18 : 1200                                                    POINT
@SUM(C15..C18
```

	A	B	C	D	E	F	G	H
3	August 1993 Profit–and–Loss Statement							
4								
5			Week 1	Week 2	Week 3	Week 4		
6			**					
7	INCOME							
8	Flight Instruction		1600	1200				
9	Charter		6200	4800				
10	Aircraft Rental		5600	7000				
11	Maintenance		8600	9200				
12	TOTAL INCOME		22000	22200				
13								
14	EXPENSES							
15	Wages		6000	6600				
16	Fuel/Oil/Parts		10300	8400				
17	Rent		2000	2000				
18	Insurance		1200	1200				
19	TOTAL EXPENSES							
20								
21	TOTAL PROFIT/LOSS		22000	22200				
22								

The cell range is C15 to C18.

The cell range is highlighted in the worksheet.

● **Note** Designating a Range with the Mouse—you can quickly highlight a range by using the mouse. With the mouse pointer in the cell that forms the upper-left corner of the range, press and hold down the left mouse button, drag the mouse pointer to the cell that forms the lower-right corner of the range, and then release the button. The range will be marked.

5. Type) to complete the formula.

```
C19:                                                      VALUE
@SUM(C15..C18)

     A        B        C        D      E      F      G      H
 3  August 1993 Profit–and–Loss Statement
 4
```

6. Press → to move the cell pointer to cell D19.

```
17  Rent                  2000     2000
18  Insurance             1200     1200
19  TOTAL EXPENSES       19500
20
21  TOTAL PROFIT/LOSS     2500    22200
22
```

The TOTAL PROFIT/LOSS cell (C21) now shows the difference between income and expenses.

7. Following the procedures in steps 1–5, create the formula @SUM(D15..D18). After you type the closing parenthesis, press → to move the cell pointer to cell E19. Your computed profit-and-loss data should now appear in cell D21.

```
17  Rent                  2000     2000
18  Insurance             1200     1200
19  TOTAL EXPENSES       19500    18200
20
21  TOTAL PROFIT/LOSS     2500     4000
22
```

Your worksheet should now look like this. (If you entered the wrong
data in any cells, don't worry—Part Two will show you how to correct
these mistakes.)

E19 :								READY
	A	B	C	D	E	F	G	H
3	August 1993 Profit–and–Loss Statement							
4								
5			Week 1	Week 2	Week 3	Week 4		
6			***					
7	INCOME							
8	Flight Instruction		1600	1200				
9	Charter		6200	4800				
10	Aircraft Rental		5600	7000				
11	Maintenance		8600	9200				
12	TOTAL INCOME		22000	22200				
13								
14	EXPENSES							
15	Wages		6000	6600				
16	Fuel/Oil/Parts		10300	8400				
17	Rent		2000	2000				
18	Insurance		1200	1200				
19	TOTAL EXPENSES		19500	18200				
20								
21	TOTAL PROFIT/LOSS		2500	4000				
22								

When you begin to develop your own worksheets, you will build your
own formulas. When you do, look through the functions in the documentation provided by Lotus to see which functions can streamline
your particular computations.

Saving Your Worksheet

Now that you've created your worksheet, you will want to save it for future editing. The work you see displayed on your screen exists only in "temporary memory" (RAM); a power failure of any sort will result in the information being totally lost. Therefore, you should record the worksheet in "permanent memory" on a hard or floppy disk. I recommend you save your worksheet every few minutes while you work in order to prevent losing a large amount of work.

Saving a New File

Let's save the worksheet you have created. (If you saved this file previously, go to Lesson 17, "Saving an Existing File.")

1. Press / or move the mouse pointer into the control panel to display the main menu. Or, select the Save icon

from any of the first five palettes. (If you use the icon, skip ahead to step 4.)

2. Select File.

Quick&Easy

3. Select Save.

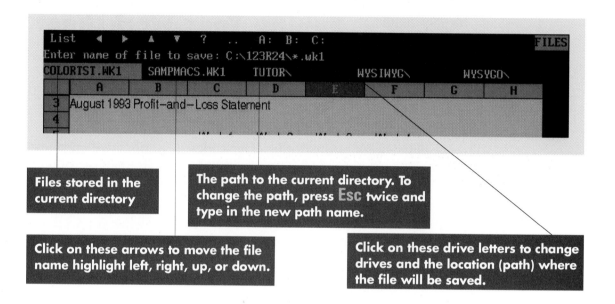

Files stored in the
current directory

The path to the current directory. To
change the path, press **Esc** twice and
type in the new path name.

Click on these arrows to move the file
name highlight left, right, up, or down.

Click on these drive letters to change
drives and the location (path) where
the file will be saved.

4. Type AUGPL1 (no file extension is needed).

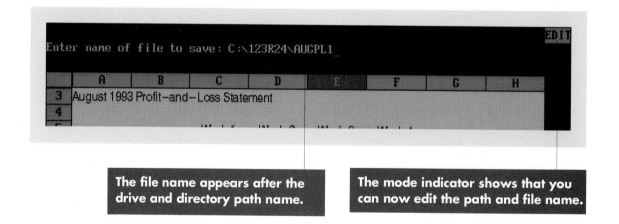

The file name appears after the
drive and directory path name.

The mode indicator shows that you
can now edit the path and file name.

● **Note** Rules for Naming Files—Use no more than eight characters.
These may be letters, numbers, a hyphen, or an underscore.
Use no blank spaces or punctuation marks.

5. Press ↵ or click the mouse button on the file name to save
the file as AUGPL1.WK1 (an abbreviated version of "AU-
GUST PROFIT/LOSS #1").

● **Note** File Extensions—A file extension appears after the file name
and consists of a period followed by up to three characters.
1-2-3 automatically gives the file extension .WK1 to any
worksheet you save, so it is not necessary to type in a file
extension when naming your files.

Note how we gave our file a descriptive file name. This will make it easier
to locate in the future.

PART TWO

Editing Your Worksheet

Now that you have learned how to construct a worksheet, let's move on to some of the basic editing and formatting features of Lotus 1-2-3. You'll change the existing data and design of the worksheet, such as correcting a value, adding a column, or deleting a row. When you finish this part, you will have all the basic skills needed to design, create, and edit worksheets.

- Retrieving a Saved File

- Correcting Your Worksheet

- Using 1-2-3's Help Feature

- Working with Columns and Rows

- Copying and Moving Data to Other Areas of the Worksheet

- Saving an Existing Worksheet

Retrieving a Saved File

9

Y ou will be using the menus a great deal in this and future lessons, so we should briefly review the procedures for selecting menu items. You can select items from the menus displayed in the control panel by pressing the first letter of the item name, or clicking on the item with the mouse pointer. You can also use the cursor keys to move the pointer to the menu item, then press ↵. You are less likely to select the wrong menu item if you use this method, but the other methods are much faster.

Selecting Menu Items

In the remaining lessons, I'll leave the selection method up to you. If you receive an instruction to select File ➤ Retrieve, you may

- simply click on the items with the mouse pointer.

- press / followed by F and R for File and Retrieve.

- use the cursor keys to position the pointer on each menu item.

- select the SmartIcon representing the menu item.

Retrieving Your Worksheet

You will often want to retrieve a saved worksheet for viewing or editing. To retrieve a file stored on a disk, you select / File ➤ Retrieve or select

the Retrieve File icon

on Palette 1.

Let's retrieve the AUGPL1.WK1 file you created in Part One.

1. Start your computer and start the 1-2-3 program, if necessary.

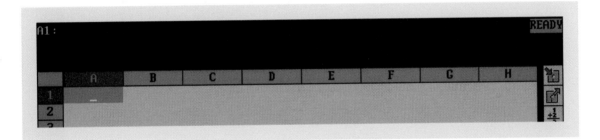

2. Select / File ➤ Retrieve, or select the Retrieve File icon. A list of files is displayed in the control panel. (If you select the Retrieve File icon, the worksheet disappears and the date, time, and file size of the highlighted file also appear in the control panel.)

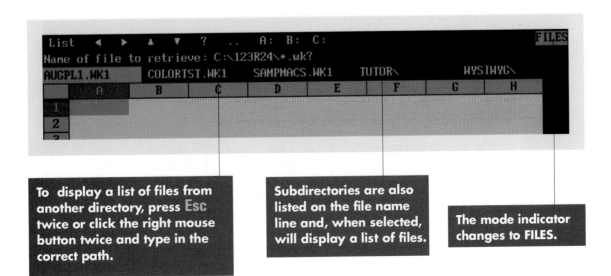

To display a list of files from another directory, press Esc twice or click the right mouse button twice and type in the correct path.

Subdirectories are also listed on the file name line and, when selected, will display a list of files.

The mode indicator changes to FILES.

3. Select AUGPL1.WK1.

	A	B	C	D	E	F	G	H
3	August 1993 Profit—and—Loss Statement							
4								
5			Week 1	Week 2	Week 3	Week 4		
6			**					
7	INCOME							
8	Flight Instruction		1600	1200				
9	Charter		6200	4800				
10	Aircraft Rental		5600	7000				
11	Maintenance		8600	9200				
12	TOTAL INCOME		22000	22200				
13								
14	EXPENSES							
15	Wages		6000	6600				
16	Fuel/Oil/Parts		10300	8400				
17	Rent		2000	2000				
18	Insurance		1200	1200				
19	TOTAL EXPENSES		19500	18200				
20								
21	TOTAL PROFIT/LOSS		2500	4000				
22								

E19 :   READY

• Note Saving Your Work—If you are working on a worksheet and want to retrieve another worksheet, save the current worksheet first. Otherwise, the current worksheet will be replaced without being saved and all your current work will be lost.

In the next lesson, you'll make some changes to the worksheet.

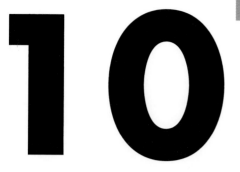

Using 1-2-3's Help Feature

1-2-3 has an on-screen Help feature that gives you a brief description of each 1-2-3 command. You may find it useful as a quick reference when you cannot remember a command key sequence.

● Note You may find it reassuring that there's help, explanations, or even advice available just a mouse-click away. This book will show you the basics but eventually you'll need some help or a quick reminder. On-screen Help is the first place you should look.

Getting Help

1. Press F1 (the Help key), or select the Help icon

on Palette 4. The 1-2-3 Main Help Index appears with the About Help menu item highlighted.

Quick **Easy**

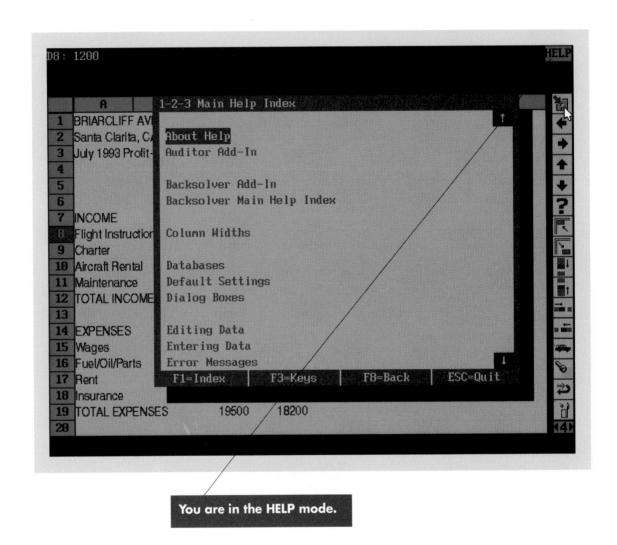

You are in the HELP mode.

2. Press ↵ or click on the About Help menu item.

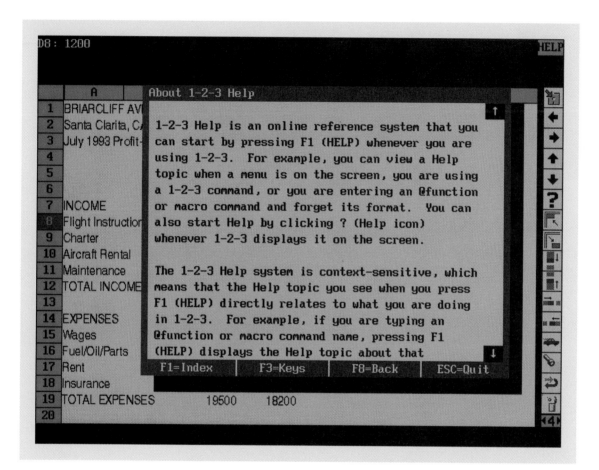

Review this screen for a brief description of how to move the highlight around the Help screens. Press ↓ or ↑, or click on the up or down arrow in the right-hand corners of the help box to scroll through the text.

3. Press **F1**, or click on F1=Index to return to the Main Help Index.

● Note Context-Sensitive Help—If you are working with a particular feature of 1-2-3 and need help, press **F1** and Help will automatically display information for that feature. (For example, if you select File ➤ Save from the menu and press **F1**, you will receive help with saving a file.) Note, however, that because the Help icon turns on the Help system only when 1-2-3 is in READY mode, there is no context-sensitive help available through the Help icon.

11

Making Corrections on Your Worksheet

When you typed labels and values in earlier lessons, you learned you could use the Backspace key to correct mistakes—provided you had not placed your entry into the worksheet. In this lesson you will learn how to correct these items *after* they are placed in a cell. You'll also learn how to erase all or part of a worksheet and to use the Undo feature to restore your worksheet to the way it was before you made an edit.

Editing Worksheet Entries

To edit the data in a cell, you must first place the cell pointer on that cell. Then, you can simply type the new entry and press ↵, overwriting the previous entry. If you have a large entry that requires a small edit, you can use this method instead: press **F2** (the Edit key) to display the current cell data in the control panel, then edit the data there.

Using these methods, let's make some changes to the AUGPL1.WK1 worksheet.

Typing in a New Entry

1. Move the cell pointer to cell C11.

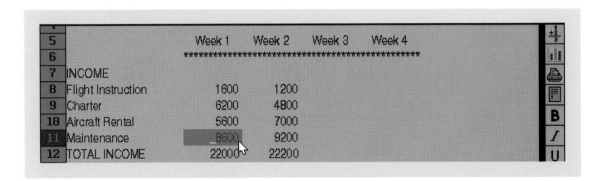

2. Type **6600**.

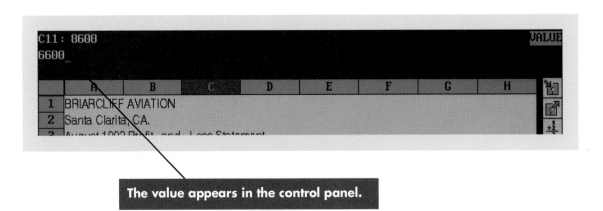

The value appears in the control panel.

3. Press ↵ to place the new value into cell C11.

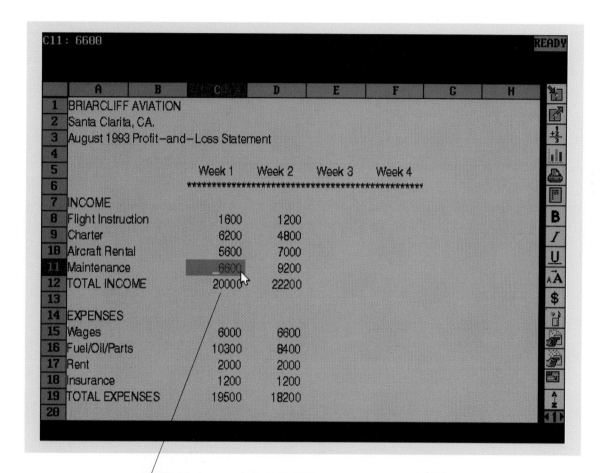

C11 : 6600   READY

	A	B	C	D	E	F	G	H
1	BRIARCLIFF AVIATION							
2	Santa Clarita, CA.							
3	August 1993 Profit–and–Loss Statement							
4								
5			Week 1	Week 2	Week 3	Week 4		
6			***					
7	INCOME							
8	Flight Instruction		1600	1200				
9	Charter		6200	4800				
10	Aircraft Rental		5600	7000				
11	Maintenance		6600	9200				
12	TOTAL INCOME		20000	22200				
13								
14	EXPENSES							
15	Wages		6000	6600				
16	Fuel/Oil/Parts		10300	8400				
17	Rent		2000	2000				
18	Insurance		1200	1200				
19	TOTAL EXPENSES		19500	18200				
20								

The TOTAL INCOME entry is automatically updated.

Using the Edit Key

Now, let's edit a longer entry using the Edit key (**F2**).

1. Move the cell pointer to cell A3 and press **F2**. The label appears in the control panel.

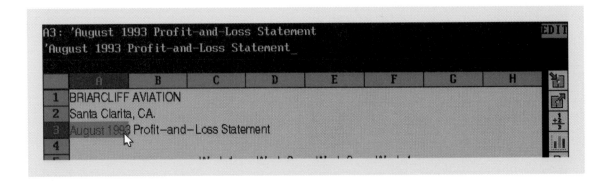

2. Press **Home**, then → to place the cursor on the *A* in *August*.

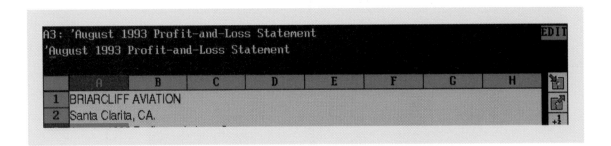

3. Press **Delete** six times and type **July**.

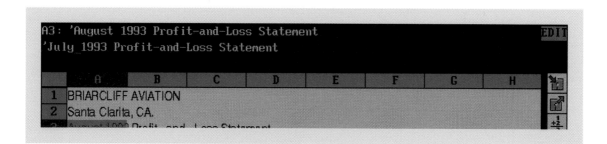

4. Press ↵ to place the edited label in cell A3.

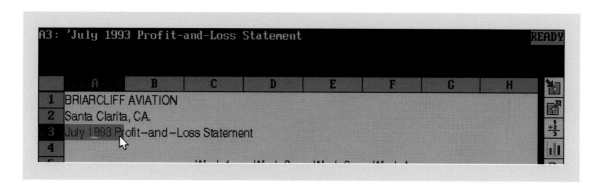

You can edit entries in the control panel using the following keys:

→	Moves cursor to right
←	Moves cursor to left
↓	Completes edit and moves cell pointer down one cell
↑	Completes edit and moves cell pointer up one cell
Backspace	Erases character to left of cursor

Delete	Erases character at cursor location
End	Moves cursor to last character
Esc	Erases entire entry
Home	Moves cursor to first character
Insert	Changes between INSERT and TYPEOVER modes

• Note Erasing Values and Labels—You cannot completely erase a value or label from a cell with F2. To delete an entire cell entry, you must use the Range ➤ Erase command. (See "Erasing Part of the Worksheet" in this lesson.)

Keep this worksheet on your screen for use in the following exercises.

Using the Undo Feature

The Undo feature is a very helpful editing tool. It returns your worksheet to the state it was in when 1-2-3 was last in READY mode. How does Undo work? Whenever you change from READY mode to a different mode, 1-2-3 creates a backup copy of your worksheet. If you edit the worksheet and make a mistake, you can use Undo to replace the botched worksheet with the unchanged backup copy.

Turning On Undo

Before you can use Undo, you must turn it on. When Undo is operating, *UNDO* appears on the status line at the bottom of the worksheet.

1. Select / Worksheet ➤ Global ➤ Default ➤ Other to display
the 1-2-3 Default Settings menu. (Default settings are automatically operating when you start the program.)

```
A3: 'July 1993 Profit-and-Loss Statement                        MENU
International  Help  Clock  Undo  Beep  Add-In  Expanded-Memory
Punctuation  Currency  Date  Time  Negative  Quit
                        Default Settings
 ┌─────────────────────────────────────────────────────────────────┐
 │    Directory: [C:\123R24·····················]  ┌─Clock─────────┐ │
 │                                                 │ (*) Standard  │ │
 │    [x] Auto-execute Macros on                   │ ( ) International│
 │    [ ] Instant access to Help file              │ ( ) None      │ │
 │    [ ] Undo on                                  │ ( ) File name │ │
 │    [ ] Enhanced expanded memory on              └───────────────┘ │
 │    [x] Computer Bell on                                           │
 │                                                                   │
 │   ┌─Auto-attach add-ins─────────────────┐    ┌─Add-in Keys─────┐  │
 │    1: [WYSIWYG·]   5: [········]         │    │ ALT-F7:  ICONS  │  │
 │    2: [ICONS···]   6: [········]  Invoke:│    │ ALT-F8:  (none) │  │
 │    3: [········]   7: [········]   (none)│    │ ALT-F9:  (none) │  │
 │    4: [········]   8: [········]         │    │ ALT-F10: (none) │  │
 │   └─────────────────────────────────────┘    └─────────────────┘  │
 │                                                                   │
 │    Configuration file: C:\123R24\123.CNF                          │
 │                                                                   │
 │            ┌───────────────────────────────────────┐             │
 │            │ Press F2 (EDIT) to edit settings       │             │
 │            └───────────────────────────────────────┘             │
 └─────────────────────────────────────────────────────────────────┘
24-Apr-92   10:31 AM
```

2. Select Undo ➤ Enable to turn on the Undo feature. Undo
will remain on until you disable it or exit 1-2-3.

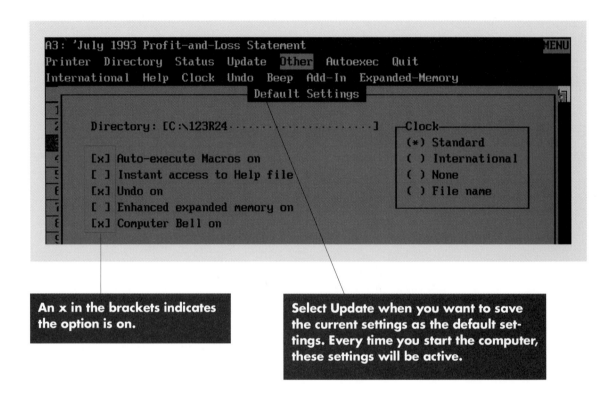

A3: 'July 1993 Profit-and-Loss Statement   MENU
Printer Directory Status Update Other Autoexec Quit
International Help Clock Undo Beep Add-In Expanded-Memory
                        Default Settings

    Directory: [C:\123R24 ·]   ┌Clock─────
                                                                     (*) Standard
    [x] Auto-execute Macros on   ( ) International
    [ ] Instant access to Help file   ( ) None
    [x] Undo on   ( ) File name
    [ ] Enhanced expanded memory on
    [x] Computer Bell on

**An x in the brackets indicates
the option is on.**

**Select Update when you want to save
the current settings as the default settings. Every time you start the computer,
these settings will be active.**

● **Note** If You Can't Activate Undo—The Undo feature requires a large
amount of temporary memory (RAM) for the backup worksheet.
If there is not enough RAM, an error message will appear when
you try to enable Undo. To make more RAM available, press F1
and follow the instructions for detaching 1-2-3 add-ins. (For
more information about add-ins, see Lesson 29.)

3. Select Quit to return to the worksheet.

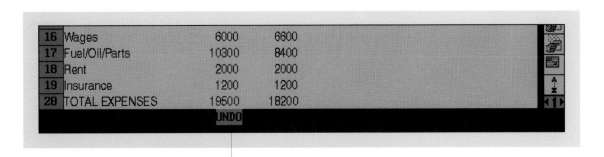

16	Wages	6000	6600
17	Fuel/Oil/Parts	10300	8400
18	Rent	2000	2000
19	Insurance	1200	1200
20	TOTAL EXPENSES	19500	18200

UNDO

UNDO appears on the status line.

Working with Undo

Let's see how Undo works.

1. Press Home to move the cell pointer to cell A1. Type **Airplanes Unlimited** and press ↵. The new label is placed in the cell.

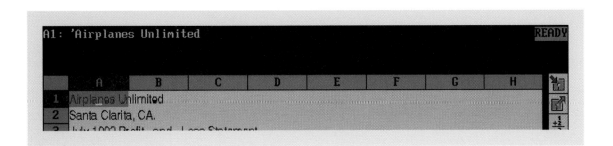

A1: 'Airplanes Unlimited   READY

	A	B	C	D	E	F	G	H
1	Airplanes Unlimited
2	Santa Clarita, CA.
3	July 1993 Profit and Loss Statement

2. Press Alt-F4 (be sure to hold Alt down while you press F4),
or select the Undo icon

on Palette 4. The previous label, BRIARCLIFF AVIATION,
is restored.

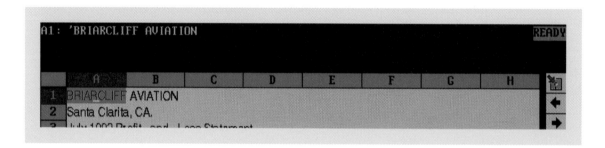

● **Note** Some Limitations of Undo—The Undo feature cannot undo
certain 1-2-3 commands, and cannot undo changes to a file
that is stored on a disk (i.e., if you delete a file from the disk,
you cannot use Undo to recover the file). Refer to your 1-2-3
documentation for a detailed explanation of the Undo
limitations.

Erasing Part of the Worksheet

Your July 1993 Profit-and-Loss Statement worksheet should be on-screen. For this exercise, we're going to assume all the income values in Week 2 are incorrect and need changing.

Using / Range ➤ Erase

Instead of editing each cell, we'll erase all the cells with the / Range ➤ Erase command and then place new values in each cell.

1. Move the cell pointer to cell D8.

2. Select Range ➤ Erase.

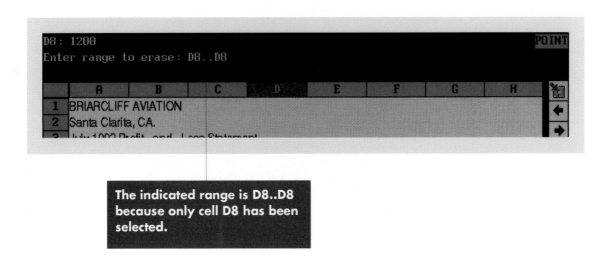

The indicated range is D8..D8 because only cell D8 has been selected.

Quick & Easy

3. Press ↓ to move the cell pointer to cell D11, or click on cell D8 and drag the pointer to cell D11.

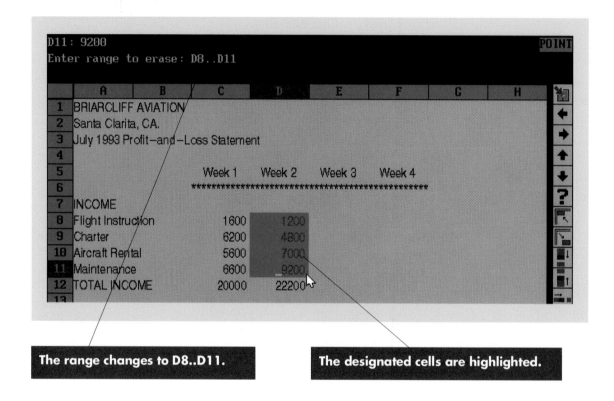

D11: 9200   POINT
Enter range to erase: D8..D11

	A	B	C	D	E	F	G	H
1	BRIARCLIFF AVIATION							
2	Santa Clarita, CA.							
3	July 1993 Profit–and–Loss Statement							
4								
5			Week 1	Week 2	Week 3	Week 4		
6			**					
7	INCOME							
8	Flight Instruction		1600	1200				
9	Charter		6200	4800				
10	Aircraft Rental		5600	7000				
11	Maintenance		6600	9200				
12	TOTAL INCOME		20000	22200				
13								

The range changes to D8..D11.

The designated cells are highlighted.

4. Press ↵ or click the left mouse button in the control panel. The range is deleted.

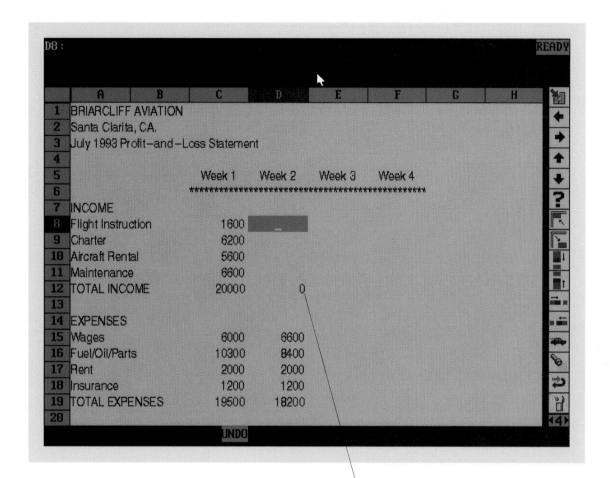

The **TOTAL INCOME** cell automatically changes.

5. Press Alt-F4, or select the Undo icon to restore the data.

5		Week 1	Week 2	Week 3	Week 4
6		**			
7	INCOME				
8	Flight Instruction	1600	1200		
9	Charter	6200	4800		
10	Aircraft Rental	5600	7000		
11	Maintenance	6600	9200		
12	TOTAL INCOME	20000	22200		
13					

● Note Selecting a Range of Data before Selecting Menu Options—For some 1-2-3 operations you can select a range of data *before* you select a menu option or SmartIcon. Then, when you select the menu option or SmartIcon, the action is automatically performed on the range. To select a range with the keyboard, press F4 and use the direction keys to highlight the desired cells; with the mouse, drag the cell pointer over the desired cells.

Using the Delete Icon

Let's take a look at how the Delete icon

is used to erase data from cells.

1. With the cell pointer in cell D8, drag the cell pointer to cell D11 with the mouse, or press **F4**, move the cell pointer to cell D11 to highlight the range D8..D11, and press ↲.

		Week 1	Week 2	Week 3	Week 4
5					
6		**
7	INCOME				
8	Flight Instruction	1600	1200		
9	Charter	6200	4800		
10	Aircraft Rental	5600	7000		
11	Maintenance	6600	9200		
12	TOTAL INCOME	20000	22200		

2. Select the Delete icon from Palette 4. The values are erased from the worksheet.

		Week 1	Week 2	Week 3	Week 4
5					
6		**
7	INCOME				
8	Flight Instruction	1600			
9	Charter	6200			
10	Aircraft Rental	5600			
11	Maintenance	6600			
12	TOTAL INCOME	20000	0		

3. Press **Alt-F4**, or select the Undo icon to restore the data. Then press **Esc** or click the right mouse button to clear the range highlight.

Erasing the Entire Worksheet

There will be times when a worksheet will need complete reorganization. When this happens, you need a way to erase the entire worksheet. You can do this with the / Worksheet ➤ Erase command.

Be sure Undo is turned on (*UNDO* will appear on the status line) so we can recover the data after it has been erased.

1. Select / Worksheet ➤ Erase.

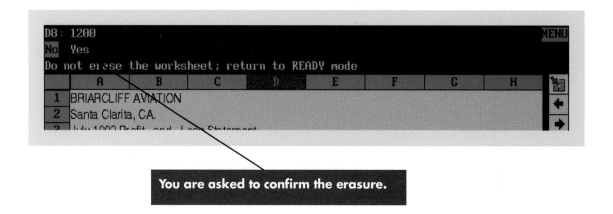

You are asked to confirm the erasure.

2. Select Yes. You are alerted that the worksheet has not been saved.

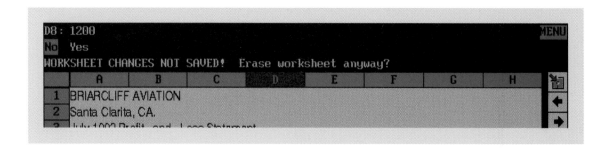

3. Select Yes. The worksheet is cleared of data.

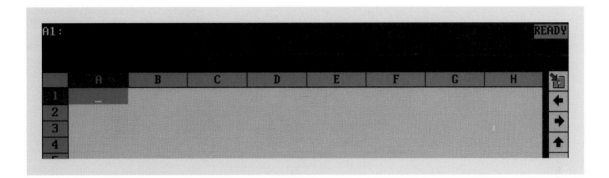

4. Press **Alt-F4**, or select the Undo icon to restore the data.

You'll use this worksheet in Lessons 12 throught 16. Should you want to stop work before Lesson 16, turn to Lesson 16 for instructions on how to save an existing file.

Performing "What If" Analyses

Whenever you change a value, 1-2-3 automatically recalculates all worksheet formulas. You can take advantage of this ability by playing the "What If" game. For example, say you want to forecast what profits you'd realize if you increased the price for maintenance or flight instruction. Or, what if your rent were raised and your parts supplier told you there would be an increase in parts prices? These questions can be answered simply by placing the anticipated price changes into the appropriate cells on your worksheet; the results of these changes will be computed automatically by 1-2-3.

10 MINUTES

Editing Columns

12

Columns are one of the major components of a worksheet. 1-2-3 enables you to change the column widths, insert new columns among existing columns, delete columns that no longer serve your purpose, and even hide columns so they can't be seen or printed.

Changing Column Widths

The default width of a 1-2-3 column is nine characters. You will at times, however, want wider or narrower columns to accommodate more or less data.

1. With the July worksheet on-screen, move the cell pointer to the Week 1 label in cell C5. (You may place the pointer in any cell in the column you want to modify.)

2. Select / Worksheet ➤ Column.

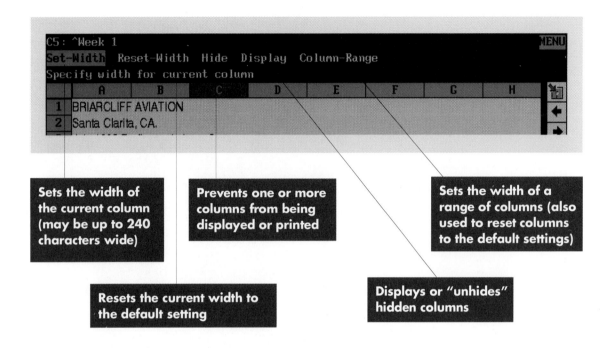

Sets the width of the current column (may be up to 240 characters wide)

Prevents one or more columns from being displayed or printed

Sets the width of a range of columns (also used to reset columns to the default settings)

Resets the current width to the default setting

Displays or "unhides" hidden columns

3. Select Set-Width.

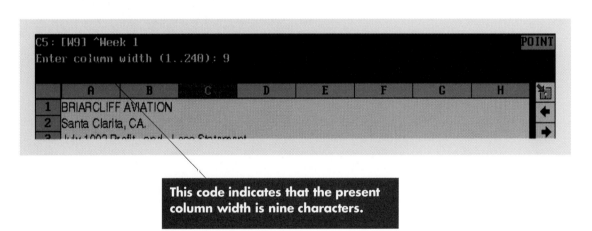

This code indicates that the present column width is nine characters.

4. Press → three times, and then press ↵. The column-width code changes to 12 and the column C width adjusts to 12 characters.

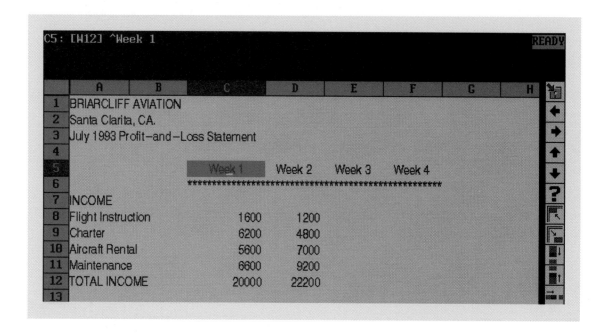

5. Select /Worksheet ➤ Column ➤ Reset-Width. This resets the column width to the default setting of nine characters.

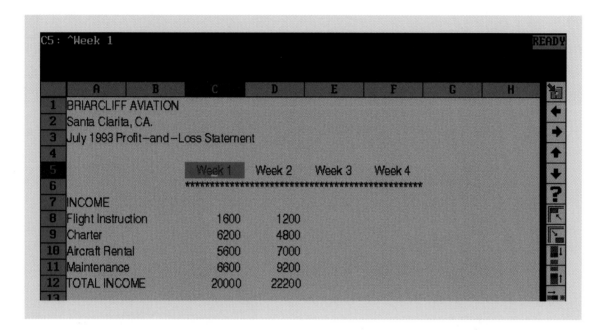

Changing a Range of Column Widths

This feature allows you to widen two or more adjacent columns at the same time. This is a speedy method of changing column widths across a large worksheet.

1. Position the cell pointer in the first column of the group of columns you wish to change (in this case, in cell C5). Select /Worksheet ➤ Column ➤ Column-Range.

2. Select Set-Width.

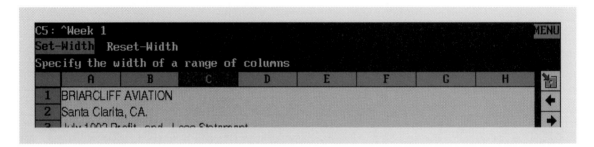

3. Press → three times, or drag the cell pointer to cell F5 to highlight cells C5 through F5.

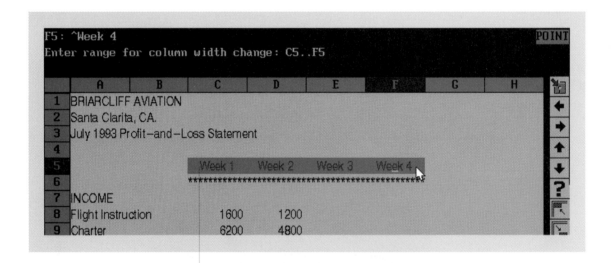

You only need to specify one cell in each column to change the entire column.

4. Press ↵, or click in the control panel.

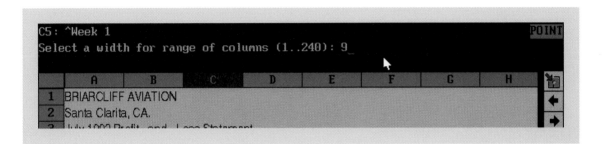

5. Type **12** and press ↵. Columns C through F are adjusted to 12 characters in width.

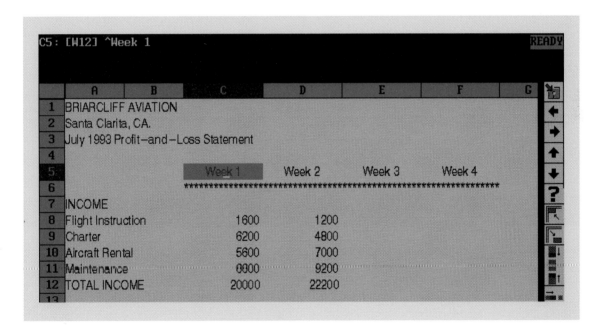

6. To reset the columns to the default width of nine characters, place the cell pointer in column C and select /Worksheet ➤ Column ➤ Column-Range ➤ Reset-Width.

7. Press → three times and press ↵, or drag the cell pointer to cell F5 and then click in the control panel. The columns automatically readjust to nine characters.

Inserting Columns

This feature allows you to add a column between existing columns. The new column can be used for data or just to alter the appearance of the worksheet.

Using /Worksheet ➤ Insert ➤ Column

Let's add some space between the income and expenses labels and the Week 1 values by adding a blank new column.

1. Move the cell pointer to cell C5 and select /Worksheet ➤ Insert.

2. Select Column. You are asked to specify the range. You may insert one or more adjacent columns.

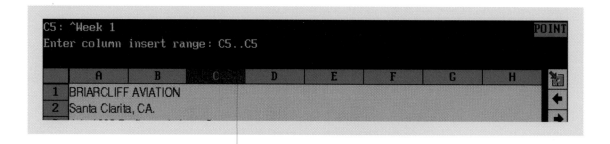

Only one column (C) is displayed in the range.

3. Press ↵ or click in the control panel to add a single new column.

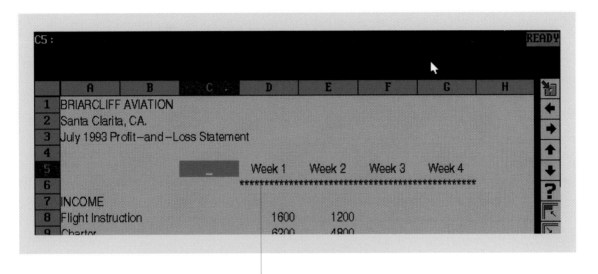

The existing columns move to the right.

Using the Insert Column Icon

Now, let's insert a column using the Insert Column icon

1. Display Palette 3.

2. Select the Insert Column icon. A second blank column is inserted in the worksheet.

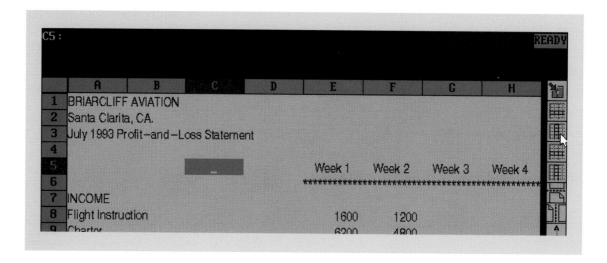

To insert a *range* of columns, drag the mouse pointer to highlight at least one cell in each column before selecting the Insert Column icon.

Deleting Columns

You can easily delete columns that are not needed. Let's delete the blank columns you just inserted.

Before you begin this exercise, be sure to save your worksheet. If you make an error, simply select Undo immediately or retrieve the saved version of the file. Remember, Undo must be turned on before you begin editing the columns.

Using /Worksheet ➤ Delete ➤ Column

1. With the cell pointer located in cell C5, select /Worksheet ➤ Delete.

2. Select Column.

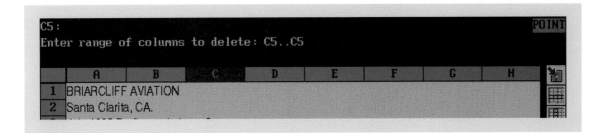

3. Click in the control panel or press ↵ to accept the C5..C5 range. Column C is deleted and the remaining columns move to the left to fill the empty space.

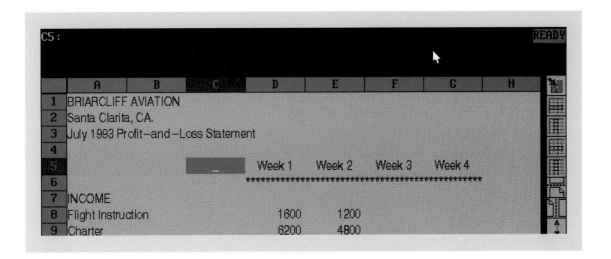

Using the Delete Column Icon

Now, let's delete a column using the Delete Column icon

The cell pointer should be in cell C5.

1. Display Palette 3 and select the Delete Column icon. You are given the option to cancel the deletion in case you are deleting the wrong column.

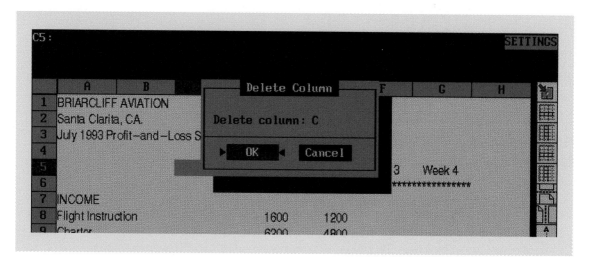

2. Select OK. The column disappears.

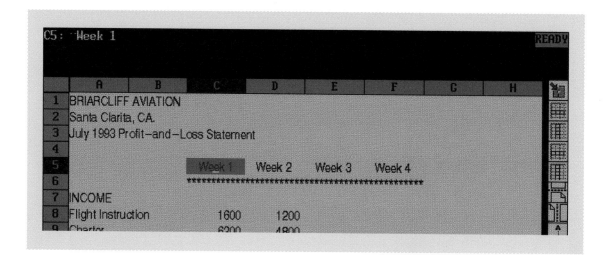

To delete a *range* of columns, drag the mouse pointer to highlight at least one cell in each column, or press **F4**, highlight at least one cell in each column, and press ↲. Then, select the Delete Column icon.

● Note | Deleting Columns and Rows—A column or row is deleted in its entirety from the top (left) of the worksheet to the bottom (right), and any data contained in a column or row is lost when the column (or row) is deleted. When working on a larger worksheet, be careful not to delete data that is in the column or row but is not displayed on the screen. You will not be able to delete columns if the /Worksheet ➤ Global ➤ Protection is enabled.

Hiding Columns

If you work with sensitive data, there may be times when you don't want other people to see information displayed on your screen. With 1-2-3, you can hide one or more columns. The hidden information will not print, but the worksheet formulas that use data in the hidden columns will continue to work properly.

Let's hide columns D, E, and F on your worksheet.

1. Place the cell pointer in cell D5 and select /Worksheet ➤ Column.

2. Select Hide.

3. Highlight the range D5..F5.

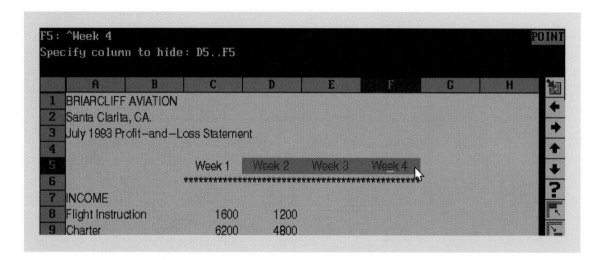

4. Click in the control panel or press ↵. Columns D through F disappear from the display.

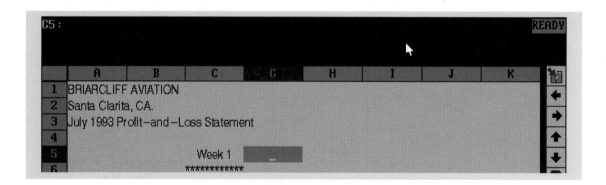

Redisplaying Columns

Now, let's redisplay the hidden columns.

1. Select /Worksheet ➤ Column.

2. Select Display.

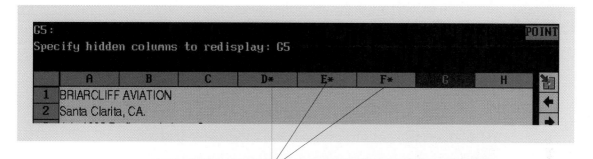

When 1-2-3 changes to **POINT** mode, hidden columns are designated with an asterisk (*) next to the column letters.

3. Type **d5..f5** or use the mouse to highlight the range.

4. Click in the control panel or press ↵. The columns are no longer hidden from view.

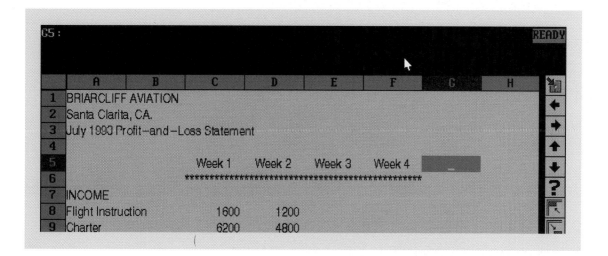

• Note Using Undo with Hidden Columns—If you redisplay your columns and immediately realize you want them hidden again, press Alt-F4 or select the Undo icon *before doing anything else.* The columns will immediately return to HIDDEN mode.

13

Editing Rows

You can use the same powerful tools we worked with in the last lesson to edit rows of data. This lesson will show you how to insert and delete rows in your worksheet.

Inserting Rows

Let's insert a blank row to put some space between the weekly column headings and the income data on the July worksheet.

Using /Worksheet ➤ Insert ➤ Row

1. With the cell pointer in cell C5, select /Worksheet ➤ Insert ➤ Row.

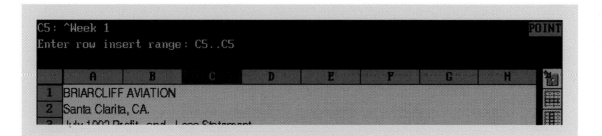

2. Press **Esc** or click the right mouse button to unanchor the range.

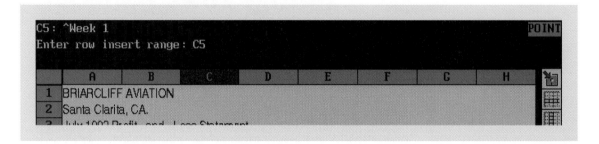

3. Move the cell pointer to the row where you want to insert the blank row (in this case, cell A7), and press ↵ or click the left mouse button in the control panel.

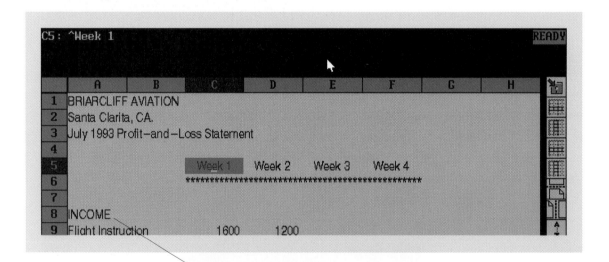

The INCOME label is now in row 8 and a blank row appears above it.

Using the Insert Row Icon

Now, let's insert a second blank row with the Insert Row icon

1. With the cell pointer in cell A7, display Palette 3.

2. Select the Insert Row icon. A new blank row is inserted into the worksheet.

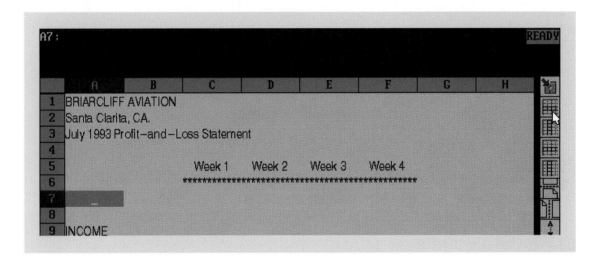

To insert a *range* of rows, drag the mouse pointer to highlight at least one cell in each row, or press **F4**, highlight at least one cell in each row, and press ⏎. Then, select the Insert Row icon.

Deleting Rows

It's as easy to delete a row as it was to insert a new row. Let's delete one of the blank rows you just inserted. Before you begin, make sure Undo is turned on.

Using /Worksheet ➤ Delete ➤ Row

1. With the cell pointer in cell A7, select /Worksheet ➤ Delete ➤ Row.

2. Press ↵ or click in the control panel. The row is deleted.

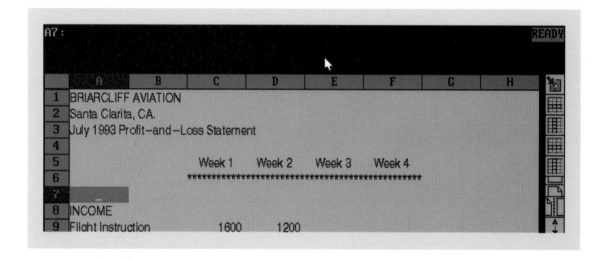

Using the Delete Row Icon

Now, let's delete the row of asterisks using the Delete Row icon

1. Move the cell pointer to any cell in the row containing asterisks. (Here, we've placed the pointer on cell C6.)

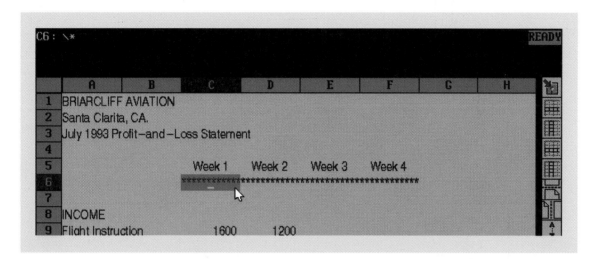

2. Display Palette 3. Then, select the Delete Row icon. You are asked to confirm the deletion.

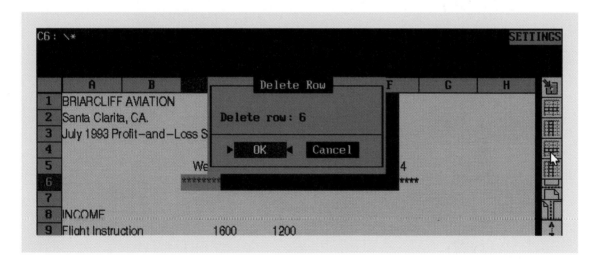

Quick&Easy

3. Select OK to complete the deletion.

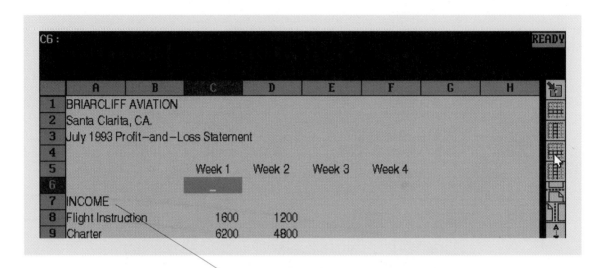

The row containing the asterisks is deleted. Notice that
the **INCOME** label moved from cell A8 to A7.

4. Press **Alt-F4** or select the Undo icon to restore the asterisks
to the worksheet.

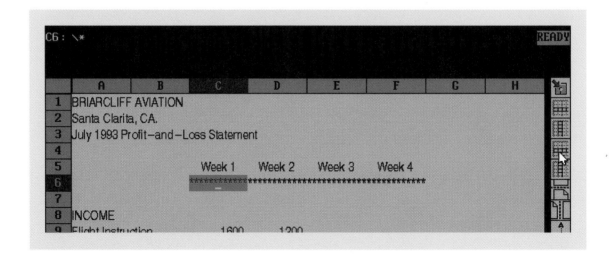

To delete a *range* of rows, drag the mouse pointer to highlight at least one cell in each row, or press F4, highlight at least one cell in each row, and press ↵. Then, select the Delete Row icon.

14

Copying and Moving Data

Y̶ou will often want to place the same data and formulas in more than one cell. The Copy command makes it possible for you to enter the data or formula once, and then place copies of this information in the appropriate cells. You can avoid going to each cell and entering the same data time after time.

There will also be times when you want to move data out of a cell or range of cells and place it elsewhere on the worksheet. The Move command works the same way the Copy command works. To move data, you can follow the instructions in this lesson, substituting Move in place of Copy and using the Move icon

instead of the Copy icon

The Copy and Move commands overwrite existing data, so you could lose important information if you aren't careful. Make sure there are enough blank cells (or cells with unwanted data) to copy or move the data into.

Copying One Cell to Another Cell

Using the July worksheet, let's copy some data from one location to another. Be sure Undo is turned on before you begin.

Using the Copy Command

1. Move the cell pointer to cell A13 and select /Copy.

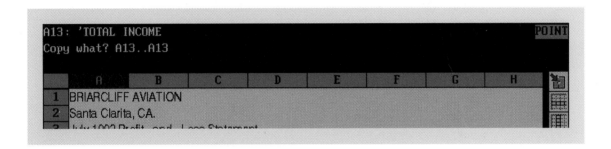

2. Press **Esc** or click the right mouse button to unanchor cell A13.

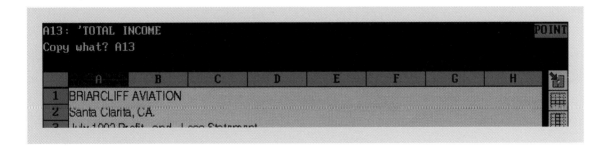

3. Move the cell pointer to cell C13. The formula totaling cells C9 through C12 appears in the control panel.

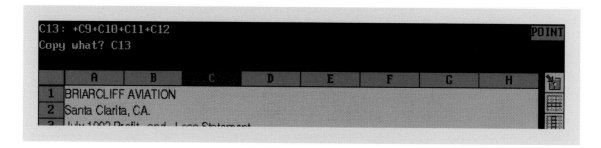

4. Press ↵ or click the left mouse button in the control panel.

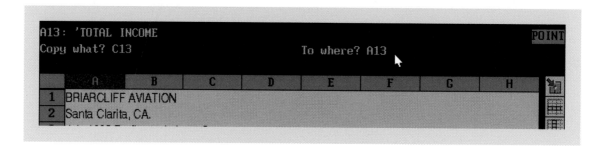

5. Move the pointer to cell E13 and click or press ↵.

		Week 1	Week 2	Week 3	Week 4
5					
6		**
7					
8	INCOME				
9	Flight Instruction	1600	1200		
10	Charter	6200	4800		
11	Aircraft Rental	5600	7000		
12	Maintenance	6600	9200		
13	TOTAL INCOME	20000	22200	0	
14					
15	EXPENSES				
16	Wages	6000	6600		
17	Fuel/Oil/Parts	10300	8400		

6. Move the pointer to cell E13.

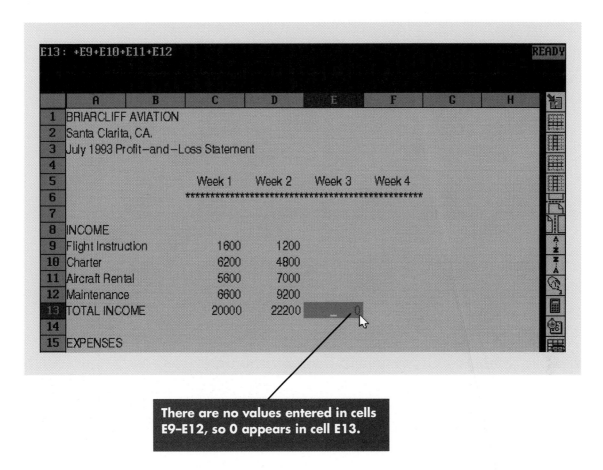

There are no values entered in cells E9–E12, so 0 appears in cell E13.

The cell addresses in the formula have changed from +C9+C10+C11+C12 to +E9+E10+E11+E12. This happened because the formula contains *relative cell addresses*—the cell names in the formula change to reflect the location of the formula (in this case, cell E13).

Using the Copy Icon

You can accomplish the same thing using the SmartIcons. The Copy icon allows you to make a *copy* of the contents of one cell and place them into another cell. The Move icon will *move* information out of a cell and place it into another.

1. With the cell pointer in cell E13, display Palette 1 and select the Copy icon. You are asked where to copy the cell.

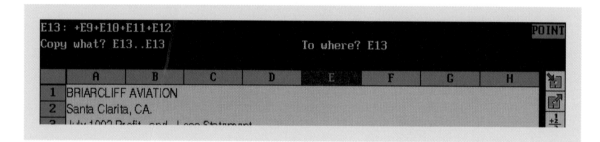

2. Move the cell pointer to cell F13 and press ↵ or click in the control panel. The formula is copied.

		Week 1	Week 2	Week 3	Week 4
5		Week 1	Week 2	Week 3	Week 4
6	***
7					
8	INCOME				
9	Flight Instruction	1600	1200		
10	Charter	6200	4800		
11	Aircraft Rental	5600	7000		
12	Maintenance	6600	9200		
13	TOTAL INCOME	20000	22200	0	0
14					
15	EXPENSES				
16	Wages	6000	6600		

3. Highlight the range E13..F13 and select the Delete icon on Palette 1 or select /Range ➤ Erase to erase the data in cells E13 and F13.

● Note Moving Formulas—If you use the Move command to move a formula from one cell to another, only the numerical value is moved, not the formula.

Copying One Cell to a Range of Cells

Remember, when you want to move the contents of one cell into a range, substitute the Move command.

Using the Copy Command

1. Move the cell pointer to cell C20.

2. Select /Copy and press ↵ or click in the control panel to accept the range. You are asked to specify the new location.

3. Move the cell pointer to cell E20 and press **Period** to anchor the first cell of the new range.

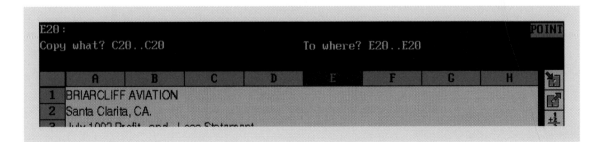

Quick&Easy

4. Drag the cell pointer to cell F20 or press → to highlight the range E20..F20.

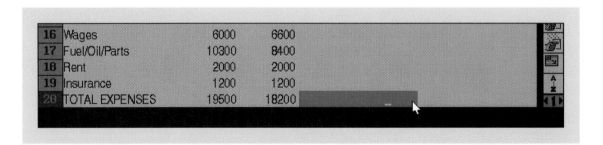

5. Press ↵ or click in the control panel to copy the formula @SUM(C16..C19) into cells E20 and F20.

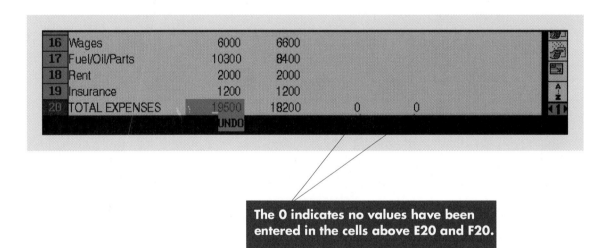

The 0 indicates no values have been entered in the cells above E20 and F20.

6. Move the cell pointer to cell E20.

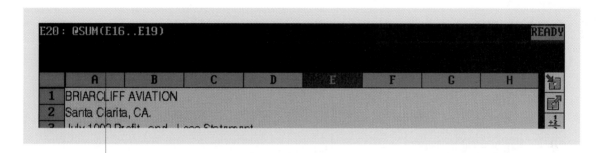

E20: @SUM(E16..E19)

READY

	A	B	C	D	E	F	G	H
1	BRIARCLIFF AVIATION							
2	Santa Clarita, CA.							

The relative references have changed to reflect the new location. Moving the pointer to cell F20 would show the formula @SUM(F16..F19).

7. Select the Undo icon, or press **Alt-F4** to restore the worksheet to its previous state.

Using the Copy Icon

Let's use the Copy icon to copy information from one cell to another cell.

107

1. With the cell pointer in cell C20, display Palette 1 and select the Copy icon. You are asked where the cell data is to be copied.

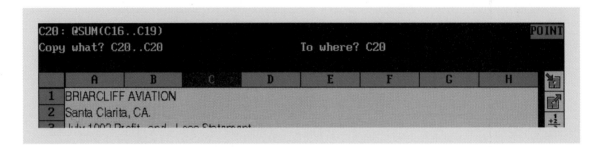

2. Move the cell pointer to cell E20, press **Period**, and highlight the range E20..F20.

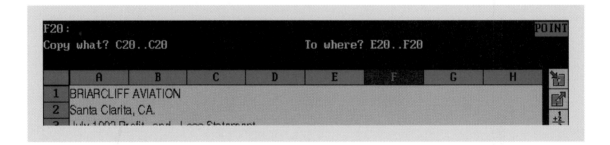

3. Press ↵ or click in the control panel. The data is copied into the range of cells.

16	Wages	6000	6600				
17	Fuel/Oil/Parts	10300	8400				
18	Rent	2000	2000				
19	Insurance	1200	1200				
20	TOTAL EXPENSES	19500	18200	0	0		

4. Select the Undo icon, or press **Alt-F4** to restore the worksheet to its previous state.

Copying a Range of Cells to Another Range of Cells

You can substitute Move for Copy when moving data from a range of cells into another range.

Using the Copy Command

1. With the cell pointer in cell C20, select /Copy.

2. Drag the mouse pointer or use the direction keys to highlight the range C20..D16.

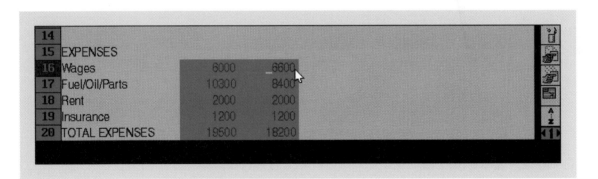

14			
15	EXPENSES		
16	Wages	6000	6600
17	Fuel/Oil/Parts	10300	8400
18	Rent	2000	2000
19	Insurance	1200	1200
20	TOTAL EXPENSES	19500	18200

3. Press ↵ or click in the control panel, and then move the pointer to cell E16.

4. Press ↵ or click in the control panel again to place the range of values and formulas into the new range.

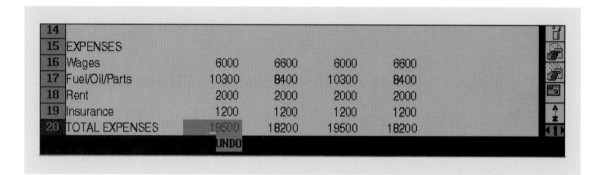

14					
15	EXPENSES				
16	Wages	6000	6600	6000	6600
17	Fuel/Oil/Parts	10300	8400	10300	8400
18	Rent	2000	2000	2000	2000
19	Insurance	1200	1200	1200	1200
20	TOTAL EXPENSES	19500	18200	19500	18200

UNDO

5. Select the Undo icon, or press **Alt-F4** to restore the worksheet to its previous state.

Using the Copy Icon

Let's copy a range of cells to another location using the Copy icon.

1. Move the cell pointer to cell C9 and highlight the range C9..D13.

2. Select the Copy icon.

3. Move the pointer to cell E9 and click or press ↵.

		Week 1	Week 2	Week 3	Week 4
5		Week 1	Week 2	Week 3	Week 4
6		***			
7					
8	INCOME				
9	Flight Instruction	1600	1200	1600	1200
10	Charter	6200	4800	6200	4800
11	Aircraft Rental	5600	7000	5600	7000
12	Maintenance	6600	9200	6600	9200
13	TOTAL INCOME	20000	22200	20000	22200
14					
15	EXPENSES				
16	Wages	6000	6600		

4. Select the Undo icon, or press **Alt-F4** to restore the worksheet to its previous state.

Working with Cell References

15

A cell name is called a *cell reference* when it forms part of a formula. A cell reference represents the value found in that specific cell. For example, in the formula @SUM(C16..C19), C16..C19 are the cell references that refer to the values in cells C16, C17, C18, and C19.

There are three types of cell references: relative, absolute, and mixed. The type of cell reference you use in a formula will determine how the formula is affected when you copy or move the formula into a different cell.

Relative References

The formulas you have created so far contain relative references—when you copied a formula from one cell to another, the cell references in the formula changed to refer to the cells at the new location. You saw an example of a relative reference formula in Lesson 14, in the section "Copying One Cell to Another Cell."

Absolute References

An absolute reference does not change to refer to a new cell when the formula is copied or moved. This is what you want when your formula should *always* refer to one specific cell value. As an example, consider a formula that calculates the interest on several different principle amounts. The interest percentage remains unchanged, or absolute, no matter if the formula is moved or copied, so the cell reference that refers to the interest percentage should be designated as an absolute reference. The interest cell reference will always refer to the one cell that contains the interest percentage.

To designate a cell reference as absolute, you type a dollar sign ($) in front of the column and row designator. For example, typing *+C3+$C$4* in cell C5 would make cell C4 an absolute reference. If you then copied this formula to cell D5, the formula would change to +D3+$C$4. The C3 entry changes to D3 because it is a relative reference, but the $C$4 entry continues to refer to the original cell location. (You'll learn more about absolute references in Part Four.)

Mixed References

A mixed reference is a single cell name that contains both a relative and an absolute reference. To understand how this works, remember that all cell names contain both a column reference and a row reference. If you wish, you can designate just one of these as an absolute reference.

For example, if you typed the cell name *$E5*, the column E portion of the name would be absolute and would not change if copied to a new cell. However, the row 5 entry *would* change. Typing the entry as E$5 works the opposite way: the column designator would change to reflect a new location, but the row designator would continue to refer to row 5. A mixed reference is helpful when you need a formula that refers to various values in a specific column, or various values in a specific row.

Saving an Existing File

16

Saving a file that has already been saved before is slightly different than saving a newly created worksheet. You can save a worksheet with a new name, or you can save a worksheet under its current name.

Saving a Worksheet with a New Name

The July worksheet should be on your screen.

1. Select the Save File icon

or select /File ➤ Save, and then press **Esc** or click the right mouse button. The current path is displayed.

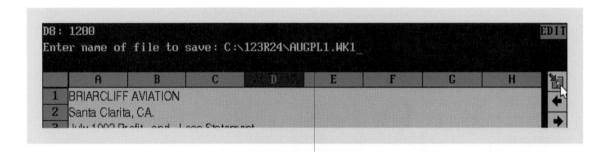

The current file name. If you want to save the file to another directory, press **Esc** three times or click the right mouse button three times (if you select the File Save icon, you must press the right mouse button five times) and type in the new drive letter, directory, and file name (i.e., **C:\DATA\JULYPL1**).

2. Type JULYPL1.

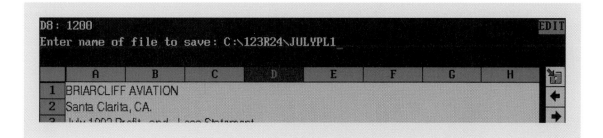

3. Press ↵ or click the left mouse button in the control panel. The file is saved with its new name (the .WK1 extension is added automatically) and you return to the worksheet.

Saving a File under Its Current Name

You will often edit and save a file using the name originally assigned to it. Let's save the JULYPL1.WK1 worksheet, which should be displayed on your screen.

1. Select the Save File icon or select /File ➤ Save, and then press ↵ or click in the control panel to accept the current path and file name.

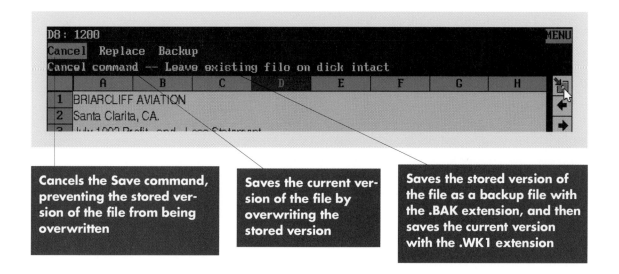

Cancels the Save command, preventing the stored version of the file from being overwritten

Saves the current version of the file by overwriting the stored version

Saves the stored version of the file as a backup file with the .BAK extension, and then saves the current version with the .WK1 extension

2. Select Replace to save the file and return to the worksheet.

 Get in the habit of saving your work frequently. If a disaster occurs, you'll then have a fairly recent version of your worksheet to start over with.

PART THREE

Formatting and Printing Your Worksheet

In this chapter you'll learn how to use 1-2-3's formatting tools. For example, you may want to format the contents of certain cells, make columns wider to accommodate more characters or to achieve a more pleasing look, or center your labels. You'll also learn how to print your worksheet.

- Adjusting Worksheet Column Widths

- Formatting Cell Values

- Assigning Names to Worksheet Data

- Creating Fixed Titles

- Positioning Labels Within Columns

- Printing a Worksheet

Changing Column Widths

17

In Lesson 12 you learned how to widen a single column. That's great, but what if you need to widen *all* the worksheet columns? You may need to do this when you want to include a currency sign, decimal point, and commas in your values, or if you are dealing with numbers that contain more than nine characters. (When a value's length exceeds the cell width, 1-2-3 displays the value in scientific notation.)

Let's widen all the columns on the AUGPL1 worksheet from nine characters to 12 characters.

1. Retrieve the file AUGPL1.WK1 and press **Home** to move the cell pointer to cell A1.

2. Select /Worksheet ➤ Global.

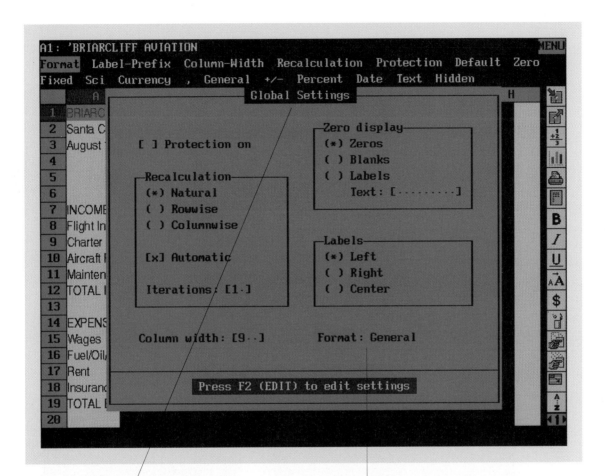

The Global Settings screen displays the current settings for the entire worksheet.

The default General cell-display format is active. This format has no comma separator, displays a minus sign with negative numbers, and has no trailing zeros to the right of the decimal point.

3. Select Column-Width.

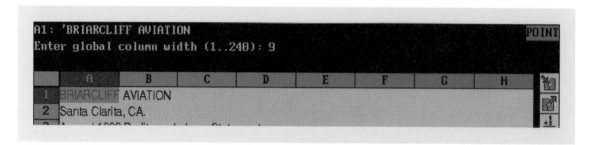

4. Type **12** or press → to expand the cell width to 12 characters, and then press ↵ or click in the control panel.

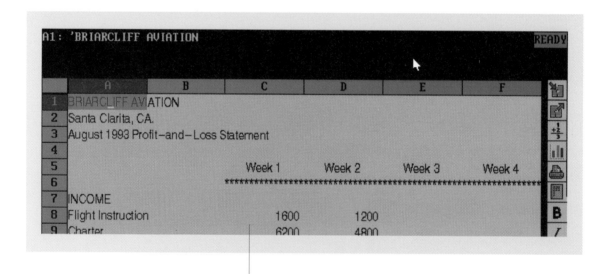

There is now space for 12 characters
in every cell on the worksheet.

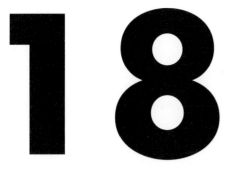

Formatting Cell Values

When you format a cell value, you specify how the value will be displayed on the screen. There are ten cell formatting options available: General, Currency, Commas, Percent, Fixed, Scientific, + and −, Date, Text, and Hidden. The cell format you've used so far is the General format—no commas, dollar signs, trailing zeros, or decimal points.

In this lesson, you'll learn how to place commas and dollar signs in the values in your AUGPL1.WK1 worksheet. (Be sure to first complete Lesson 17—all the column widths should be 12 characters.)

Formatting Your Entire Worksheet

1. With your AUGPL1.WK1 worksheet on the screen and Undo on, select /Worksheet ➤ Global.

Quick&Easy

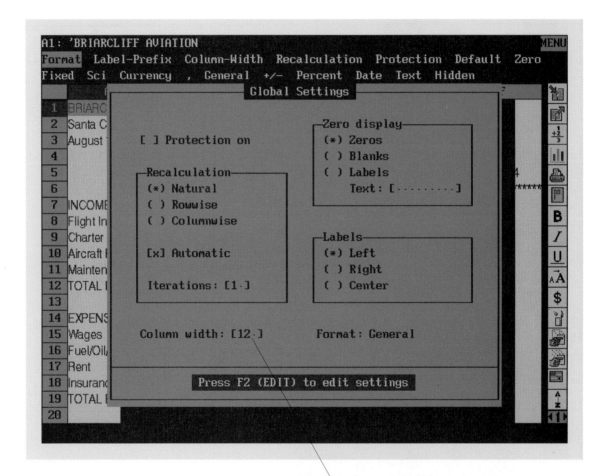

The column width is recorded on
the Global Settings screen.

2. Select Format.

3. Select , (comma) to set the number of decimal places displayed and to include commas.

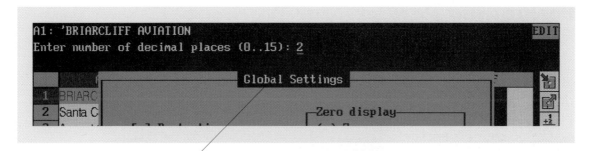

```
A1: 'BRIARCLIFF AVIATION                                          EDIT
Enter number of decimal places (0..15): 2
                              Global Settings
   1  BRIARC                                              ─Zero display─
   2  Santa C
```

You may specify up to 15 decimal places.

4. Press ↵ or click the mouse pointer on the number 2 to accept two decimal places. All the values on the worksheet now contain commas and decimal points.

```
A1: 'BRIARCLIFF AVIATION                                          READY

          A          B          C          D          E          F
   1  BRIARCLIFF AVIATION
   2  Santa Clarita, CA.
   3  August 1993 Profit-and-Loss Statement
   4
   5                            Week 1     Week 2     Week 3     Week 4
   6             ************************************************************
   7  INCOME
   8  Flight Instruction         1,600.00   1,200.00
   9  Charter                    6,200.00   4,800.00
  10  Aircraft Rental            5,600.00   7,000.00
  11  Maintenance                8,600.00   9,200.00
  12  TOTAL INCOME              22,000.00  22,200.00
  13
  14  EXPENSES
  15  Wages                      6,000.00   6,600.00
  16  Fuel/Oil/Parts            10,300.00   8,400.00
  17  Rent                       2,000.00   2,000.00
  18  Insurance                  1,200.00   1,200.00
  19  TOTAL EXPENSES            19,500.00  18,200.00
  20
                           UNDO
```

Formatting Part of Your Worksheet

Now, let's place dollar signs in the TOTAL PROFIT/LOSS row.

1. Move the cell pointer to cell C21 and select /Range ➤ Format.

2. Select Currency.

3. Press ↵ or click on the number 2 to select two decimal places. You are asked for the range of values to be formatted.

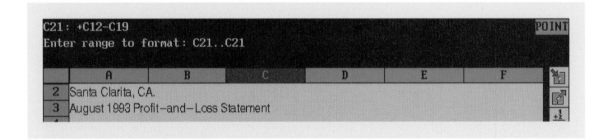

4. Press → or drag the mouse pointer to highlight the range C21..D21.

5. Press ↵ or click in the control panel.

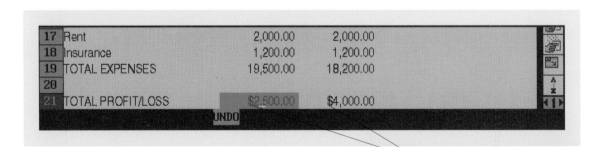

The range of cells C21 through D21 now displays dollar signs.

6. Press Alt-F4 or select the Undo icon to remove the currency signs.

Now, let's format these same cells with currency signs using the Currency Format icon

The cell pointer should be in cell C21.

1. Display Palette 2.

2. Select the range C21..D21.

3. Select the Currency Format icon. The currency symbols appear.

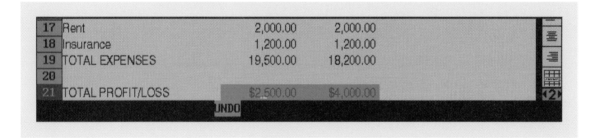

4. Return to Palette 1.

5 MINUTES

Assigning Names to Data 19

With 1-2-3, you can name values or formulas in a range of cells. This allows you to treat the range as a unit—you can use the range name instead of the cell addresses when printing, copying, moving, erasing, formatting, or using the GoTo (F5) key. (You can also assign names to single cells.)

Naming a Range

Let's assign a range name to cells A5 through D12, the INCOME portion of the AUGPL1.WK1 worksheet. Then, we'll copy the INCOME range into another location on the worksheet.

1. Move the cell pointer to cell A5.

2. Select /Range ➤ Name. You see five options for naming and working with ranges.

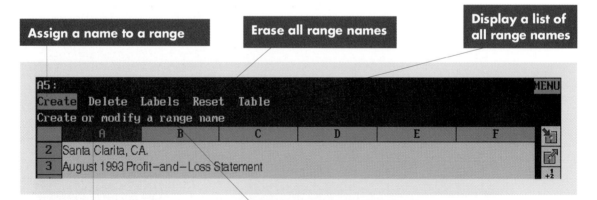

Assign a name to a range

Erase all range names

Display a list of all range names

Delete a range name

Assign range names to single-cell ranges, using adjacent labels as the range names

3. Select Create, type **INCOME**, and press ↵. You are asked to enter the range of cells.

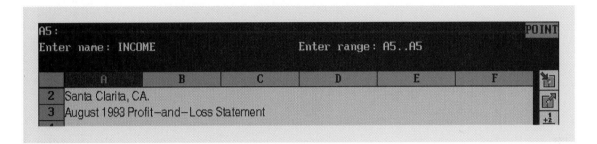

4. Highlight the range A5..D12.

5. Press ↵ or click in the control panel to complete naming the range.

Working with a Named Range

Now, let's copy this range of data to another location on the worksheet.

1. Press → to move the cell pointer to cell H5.

2. Select /Copy and type **INCOME** to specify the range of data to be copied.

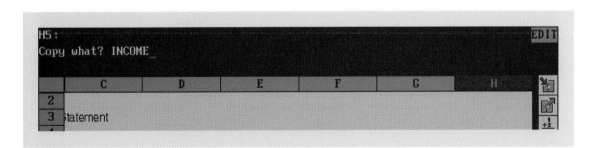

3. Press ↵ or click in the control panel.

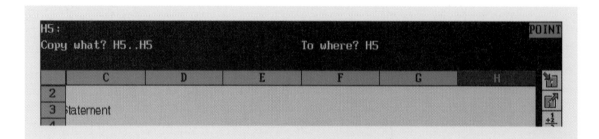

4. Press ↵ or click in the control panel again. Then move the cell pointer to cell L5. The data in the INCOME range is copied.

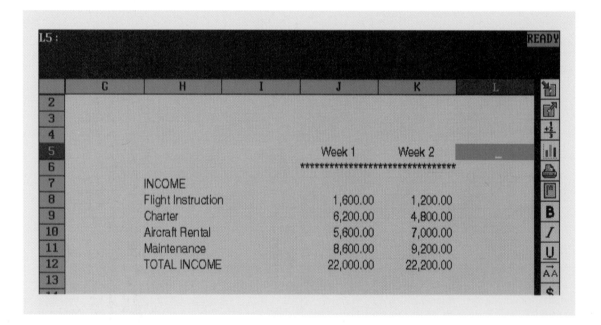

5. Press **Alt-F4** or select the Undo icon to restore the worksheet to its previous state.

Creating Fixed Titles

As you know, when you move the pointer beyond the columns or rows currently displayed, those columns and rows start to scroll off the screen, out of sight. When the column and row labels scroll off the screen, this can cause difficulties. 1-2-3's /Worksheet ➤ Titles feature allows you to fix labels (and values, if you wish) so they remain displayed at all times.

You may fix any row and column titles that border the top and/or left edges of your worksheet. You may fix titles horizontally, vertically, or both. Let's try each of these methods.

Fixing Horizontal Titles

1. With Undo on, place the pointer in cell A6 of your AUGPL1.WK1 worksheet. (You will always place the pointer in one of the cells below the rows you want to fix into place.)

2. Select /Worksheet ➤ Titles.

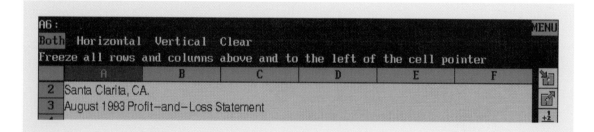

3. Select Horizontal, then move the pointer to cell A30.

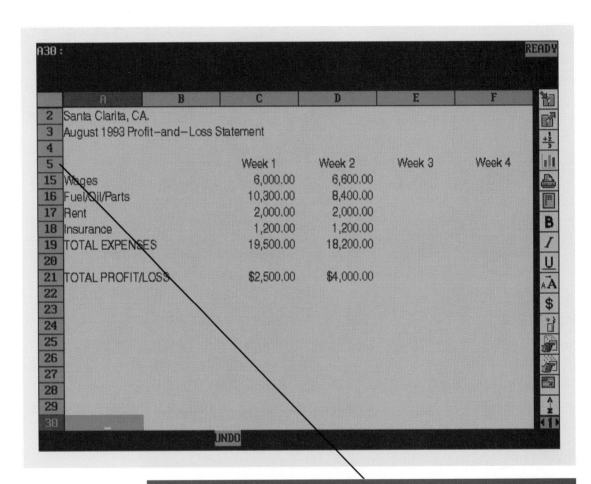

The titles from row 5 and above remain fixed in place. Rows 6 through 14 disappear from view.

Fixing Vertical Titles

When fixing vertical titles, always place the pointer one column to the right of the columns you want to fix.

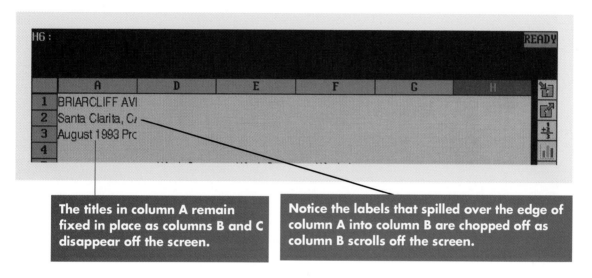

The titles in column A remain fixed in place as columns B and C disappear off the screen.

Notice the labels that spilled over the edge of column A into column B are chopped off as column B scrolls off the screen.

1. Press Home and move the pointer to cell B6.

2. Select /Worksheet ➤ Titles ➤ Vertical, and then press → to move the pointer to cell H6.

Fixing Horizontal and Vertical Titles Simultaneously

1. To fix all the titles (rows and columns) above row 13 and to the left of column E, press Home and move the pointer to cell E13.

2. Select /Worksheet ➤ Titles ➤ Both. Then, use the direction keys to move the pointer to cell I29.

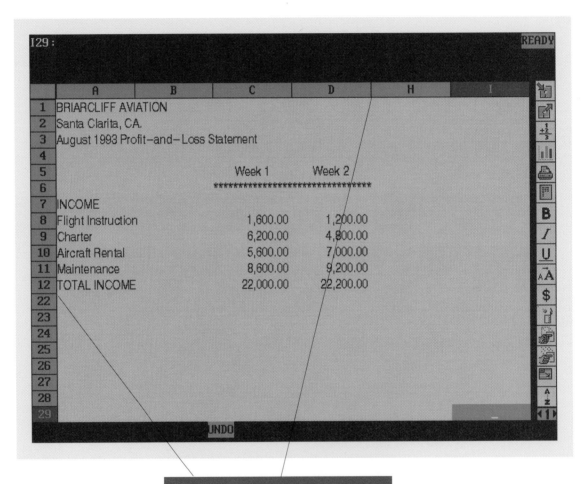

Rows 13 through 21 and columns E through G scroll off the screen.

Editing a Worksheet with Fixed Titles

You can move the pointer into an area of fixed titles only with the GoTo key or icon. Let's suppose you want to edit cell A6, which is in the fixed area of the worksheet.

1. Press F5, or display Palette 4 and click on the GoTo icon.

2. Type **A6** and press ↵. A copy of the worksheet is placed outside the fixed titles range so it can be edited.

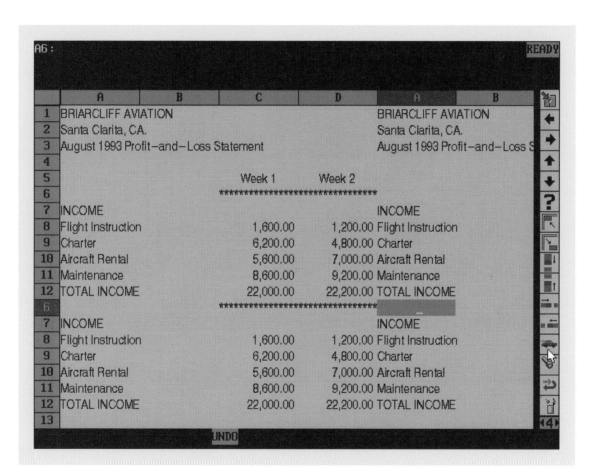

If you wanted to remove the second copy of the worksheet, you would press PageUp until all extra rows disappeared, then press PageDown until 1-2-3 beeped. You would then press Ctrl-→ until the extra columns disappeared, and finally press Ctrl-← until 1-2-3 beeped again.

Clearing Fixed Titles

1. Select /Worksheet ▶ Titles.

2. Select Clear.

21

Positioning Labels

To change the position of your worksheet labels within their respective cells, you can edit them one at a time, or you can use the /Range ➤ Label command to shift an entire range of labels. Using this command, you can align text with the left or right edge of a cell, or center it within a cell.

Using /Range ➤ Label

On your AUGPL1.WK1 worksheet, let's shift the Week 1 through Week 4 labels from the center position to the right-aligned position.

1. With Undo on and the pointer in cell A6, select /Range ➤ Label ➤ Right.

2. Type **C5..F5** and press ↵, or drag the mouse pointer from cell C5 to cell F5 and click.

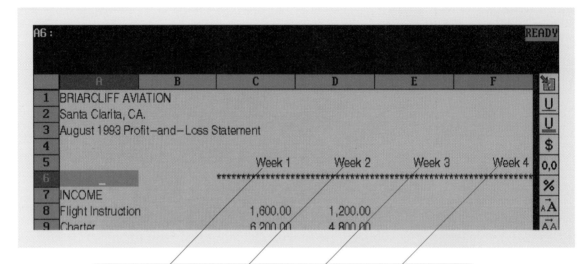

The labels move to the right edge of their respective cells.

Using the Align Icons

Now, let's use the Center Align icon

to position a range of labels in the center of their respective cells. These instructions also apply to the Right Align icon

and the Left Align icon

1. Move the cell pointer to cell C5.

2. Highlight the range C5..F5.

3. From Palette 2, select the Center Align icon. The labels are repositioned.

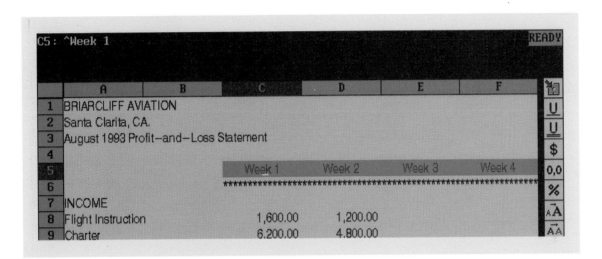

4. Click on the Save File icon and select Replace to save the file with its current name, or select /File ➤ Save, press ↵, and select Replace.

Printing Your Worksheet

22

After you have created and formatted your worksheet, you may want to print a copy of it. This lesson introduces the basics of printing a worksheet.

Display your AUGPL1 worksheet on your screen. Turn on your printer and line up the top edge of the paper with the print head.

1. Select /Print.

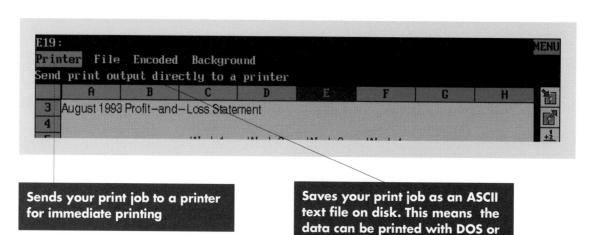

Sends your print job to a printer for immediate printing

Saves your print job as an ASCII text file on disk. This means the data can be printed with DOS or a print utility program. The text file will have a .PRN extension

2. Select Printer.

```
E19:                                                              MENU
Range  Line  Page  Options  Clear  Align  Go  Quit
Specify a range to print
┌───────────────────────── Print Settings ─────────────────────────┐
│                                                                   │
│   Range: [···············]       ┌─Destination─────────────       │
│                                  │ (*) Printer    ( ) Encoded file │
│   ┌─Margins─────────────         │ ( ) Text file  ( ) Background   │
│   │ Left:  [4··] Top:    [2·]    │                                 │
│   │ Right: [76·] Bottom: [2·]    │ File name: [···············]    │
│   ┌─Borders─────────────                                           │
│   │ Columns: [···········]        Page length: [66·]               │
│   │ Rows:    [···········]                                         │
│                                   Setup string: [············]     │
│                                                                   │
│   Header: [····························]    [ ] Unformatted pages   │
│   Footer: [····························]    [ ] List entries        │
│ ─────────────────────────────────────────────────────────────    │
│   Interface: Parallel 1            Name: HP LaserJet series        │
│                                                                   │
│         Press F2 (EDIT) to edit settings                          │
└───────────────────────────────────────────────────────────────────┘
22
```

You must always select the range of cells you want to print.

The default left margin is 4 spaces from the left edge of the paper; the right margin is 76 spaces. The top and bottom margins are 2 lines from the top and bottom of the page. The page length is 66 lines.

Print settings are the formatting commands that determine what your printed worksheet will look like.

3. Select Range.

4. Press **Home** to move the pointer to cell A1, then press **Period** to anchor cell A1 in the range.

5. Move the pointer to cell F21 to highlight the range of cells to be printed.

```
F21: (C2)                                                          POINT
Enter print range: A1..F21
```

	A	B	C	D	E	F
2	Santa Clarita, CA.					
3	August 1993 Profit-and-Loss Statement					
4						
5			Week 1	Week 2	Week 3	Week 4
6			*********	*********	*********	*********
7	INCOME					
8	Flight Instruction		1,600.00	1,200.00		
9	Charter		6,200.00	4,800.00		
10	Aircraft Rental		5,600.00	7,000.00		
11	Maintenance		8,600.00	9,200.00		
12	TOTAL INCOME		22,000.00	22,200.00		
13						
14	EXPENSES					
15	Wages		6,000.00	6,600.00		
16	Fuel/Oil/Parts		10,300.00	8,400.00		
17	Rent		2,000.00	2,000.00		
18	Insurance		1,200.00	1,200.00		
19	TOTAL EXPENSES		19,500.00	18,200.00		
20						
21	TOTAL PROFIT/LOSS		$2,500.00	$4,000.00		

6. Press ↵ to return to the Print Settings menu.

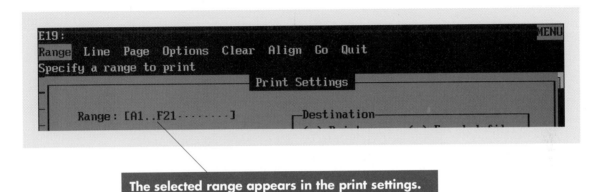

The selected range appears in the print settings.

7. Select Align to tell 1-2-3 that the printer paper is aligned with the print head. If you use a LaserJet printer, see the Note below.

● Note Printing with a LaserJet—If the page length setting on the 1-2-3 Print Settings screen is greater than the page length defined on the LaserJet control panel (the FORM option), printing after the first page will start further down on the paper. The FORM setting on a LaserJet printer is often set at 60 lines, while the default setting for 1-2-3 is 66 lines. To prevent this "creep down," select Page Length and type 60 to change the 1-2-3 setting from 66 to 60 lines. Appendix E of your 1-2-3 documentation provides more advanced information on using a LaserJet printer.

8. Select Go to print the worksheet. If you use a LaserJet printer, you must select Page to advance the paper in the printer to the top of the next page. Your printout should look like this:

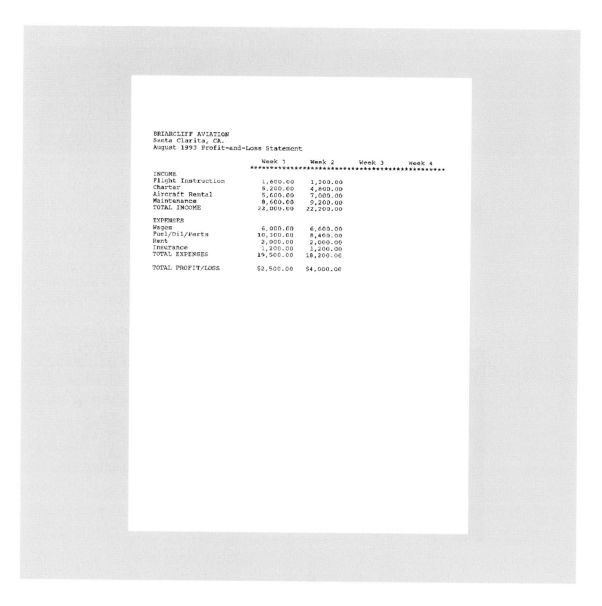

```
BRIARCLIFF AVIATION
Santa Clarita, CA.
August 1993 Profit-and-Loss Statement

                      Week 1      Week 2      Week 3      Week 4
                   ***************************************************
INCOME
Flight Instruction    1,600.00    1,200.00
Charter               6,200.00    4,800.00
Aircraft Rental       5,600.00    7,000.00
Maintenance           8,600.00    9,200.00
TOTAL INCOME         22,000.00   22,200.00

EXPENSES
Wages                 6,000.00    6,600.00
Fuel/Oil/Parts       10,300.00    8,400.00
Rent                  2,000.00    2,000.00
Insurance             1,200.00    1,200.00
TOTAL EXPENSES       19,500.00   18,200.00

TOTAL PROFIT/LOSS    $2,500.00   $4,000.00
```

9. Select Quit to return to your worksheet.

PART FOUR

Working with Advanced Calculations

You should now feel confident creating your own worksheets. This chapter introduces some additional features of Lotus 1-2-3 that you will find useful when working with your spreadsheet data. Once you've added these tools to your bag of skills you'll be able to take greater advantage of 1-2-3's ability to create professional-quality spreadsheets.

- Working with Automatic and Manual Recalculation

- Creating Absolute Formulas

- Solving "What If" Problems with Backsolver

Working with Automatic and Manual Recalculation

23

Whenever you enter or edit a cell value that is part of a formula, 1-2-3 automatically recalculates the formula and gives you updated results. If you have a large worksheet with many formulas, recalculation can take a long time. If so, you'll want to turn automatic recalculation off by turning manual recalculation on, and take control of when 1-2-3 recalculates the formulas in your worksheets.

Turning On Manual Recalculation

As before, Undo should be on as a precaution.

1. Retrieve the AUGPL1.WK1 worksheet and press **Home** to place the cell pointer in cell A1.

2. Select /Worksheet ➤ Global ➤ Recalculation.

Before recalculating the selected formula, recalculates all formulas upon which that formula depends

Recalculates all formulas, starting in row 1 and moving row by row down the worksheet

Allows you to control when 1-2-3 recalculates. Activate recalculation by pressing F9 (the CALC key)

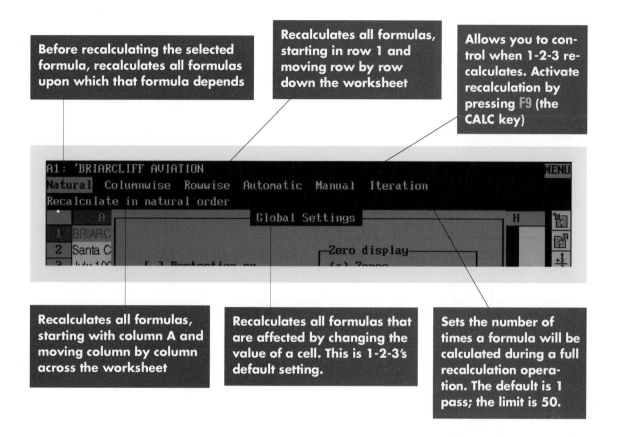

Recalculates all formulas, starting with column A and moving column by column across the worksheet

Recalculates all formulas that are affected by changing the value of a cell. This is 1-2-3's default setting.

Sets the number of times a formula will be calculated during a full recalculation operation. The default is 1 pass; the limit is 50.

3. Select Manual to turn manual recalculation on and return to the worksheet. Notice the Week 1 TOTAL INCOME is 20000.

4. Place the cursor in cell C9, type **2600**, and press ↵ to place the value.

Quick Easy

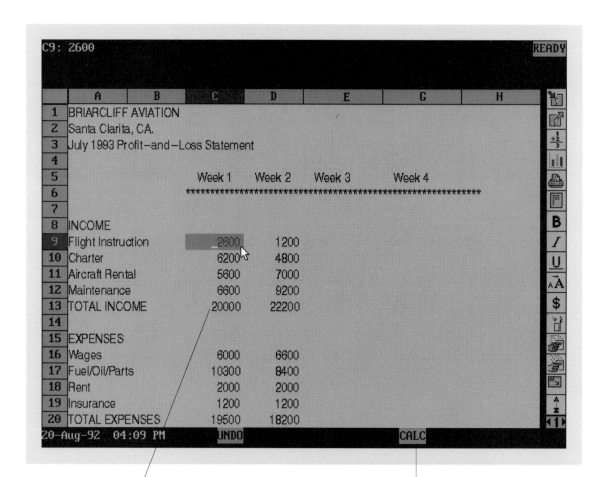

The Week 1 TOTAL INCOME value was not automatically recalculated.

The CALC indicator appears on the status line, alerting you that you're in the Manual Recalculation mode and that a change has been made to the worksheet.

5. Press F9 or select the Recalculation icon

on Palette 3.

		Week 1	Week 2	Week 3	Week 4
5					
6		**			
7					
8	INCOME				
9	Flight Instruction	2600	1200		
10	Charter	6200	4800		
11	Aircraft Rental	5600	7000		
12	Maintenance	6600	9200		
13	TOTAL INCOME	21000	22200		
14					
15	EXPENSES				
16	Wages	6000	6600		

The formula in cell C12 is recalculated and updated.

Turning On Automatic Recalculation

Let's turn the automatic recalculation feature back on.

1. Select /Worksheet ➤ Global ➤ Recalculation ➤ Automatic to turn automatic recalculation on and return to the worksheet.

2. With the pointer in cell C9, type **1600** and press ↵.

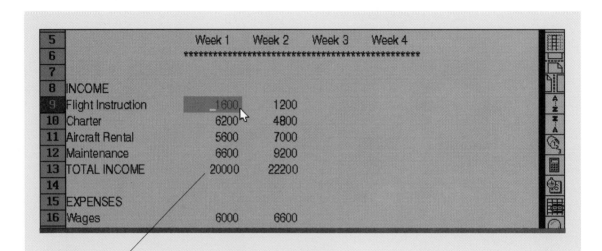

The formula is automatically recalculated
and the data is updated immediately.

24

Creating Absolute Formulas

In Part Two, you read about absolute cell references. In this lesson, I'll guide you through an example of how to create an absolute formula.

Using the JULYPL1.WK1 worksheet, let's compute the percentage of the total income represented by each income item for Week 1 and Week 2.

1. Retrieve your JULYPL1.WK1 file and move the pointer to cell G5.

2. Type **^TOTAL** and press ↓.

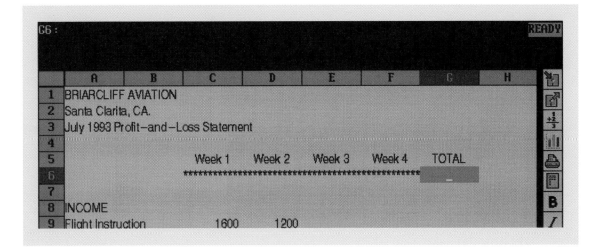

3. Type * and press ↓.

4. Move the cell pointer to cell G13, type @SUM(C13..F13), and press ↵. (Cells D13 and E13 are included in the formula range in case we want to know the totals for Week 3 and Week 4 in the future.)

	Week 1	Week 2	Week 3	Week 4	TOTAL	
5						
6	**					
7						
8 INCOME						
9 Flight Instruction	1600	1200				
10 Charter	6200	4800				
11 Aircraft Rental	5600	7000				
12 Maintenance	6600	9200				
13 TOTAL INCOME	20000	22200			42200	
14						
15 EXPENSES						
16 Wages	6000	6600				

5. Move the cell pointer to cell H5, type ^% of TOTAL, and press ↓.

6. Type * and move the cell pointer to cell H9.

7. Type @SUM(C9..F9)/$G$13.

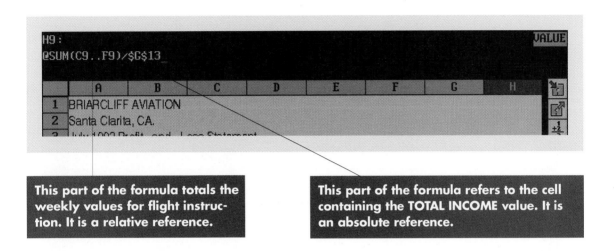

This part of the formula totals the weekly values for flight instruction. It is a relative reference.

This part of the formula refers to the cell containing the **TOTAL INCOME** value. It is an absolute reference.

8. Press ↵ or click in the control panel.

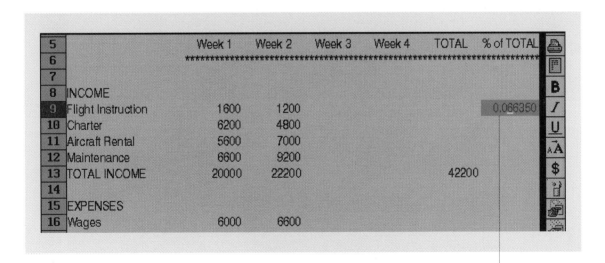

The percentage value is computed and placed in the cell. **We still need to change the cell format from General (the default) to Percent.**

9. To copy the formula in cell H9 to cells H10, H11, and H12, select Copy.

Quick & Easy

10. Press ↵ or click in the control panel to accept cell H9 as the range.

11. Type **H10..H12** and press ↵ or click in the control panel.

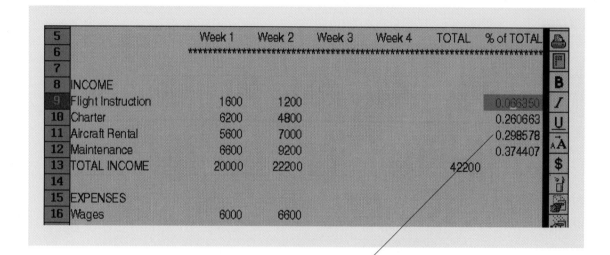

5		Week 1	Week 2	Week 3	Week 4	TOTAL	% of TOTAL
6		**
7							
8	INCOME						
9	Flight Instruction	1600	1200				0.066350
10	Charter	6200	4800				0.260663
11	Aircraft Rental	5600	7000				0.298578
12	Maintenance	6600	9200				0.374407
13	TOTAL INCOME	20000	22200			42200	
14							
15	EXPENSES						
16	Wages	6000	6600				

The formula is copied into the appropriate cells and the TOTAL INCOME percentage is computed for each income item.

If you move the cell pointer through cells H10, H11, and H12, you can see the relative reference portion of the formula change to refer to the new rows. The absolute reference portion of the formula, however, continues to refer to cell G13.

Now, let's change the decimals to percentages.

1. Place the cell pointer in cell H9 and select /Range ➤ Format ➤ Percent. Then type **0** and press ↵.

2. Highlight the range H9..H12 and press ↵. The decimals change to percentages.

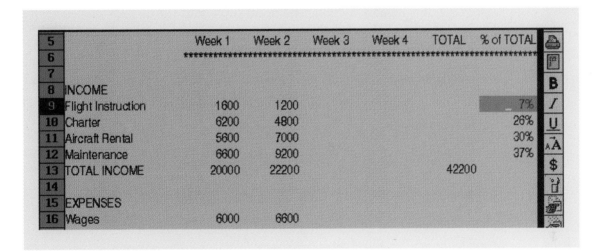

	Week 1	Week 2	Week 3	Week 4	TOTAL	% of TOTAL
5						
6	**					
7						
8 INCOME						
9 Flight Instruction	1600	1200				7%
10 Charter	6200	4800				26%
11 Aircraft Rental	5600	7000				30%
12 Maintenance	6600	9200				37%
13 TOTAL INCOME	20000	22200			42200	
14						
15 EXPENSES						
16 Wages	6000	6600				

> **● Note** Using the Percentage Format Icon—The Percentage Format icon (shown below) is on Palette 2. Before selecting the icon, select the range of values to be converted into percentages. The percentages will be displayed with two decimal points (the default).

3. Save the worksheet under the current name.

5 MINUTES

Solving "What If" Problems with Backsolver

25

In Lesson 11 you read about how you can perform "what if" analyses simply by changing one or more values and watching as 1-2-3 automatically recalculates the formula. Backsolver allows you to do the reverse—you can specify the result you want by changing the value of the *formula,* then command 1-2-3 to compute how one or more selected values in the formula must change in order to arrive at the new result.

In this lesson we will specify a new value for the TOTAL INCOME for Week 1 on the AUGPL1.WK1 worksheet, and then see how much income will be needed from flight instruction to arrive at the new TO-TAL INCOME.

Attaching Backsolver

Backsolver is an add-in program that must be attached (loaded into memory) before it can be put to use. After the program is attached it must be *invoked,* or activated. Let's see how this is done using the AUGPL1.WK1 worksheet. (Undo should be on, or you should be sure to save the worksheet before using Backsolver.)

1. Retrieve the AUGPL1.WK1 worksheet and press Home to move the cell pointer to cell A1.

2. Select /Add-In from the main menu.

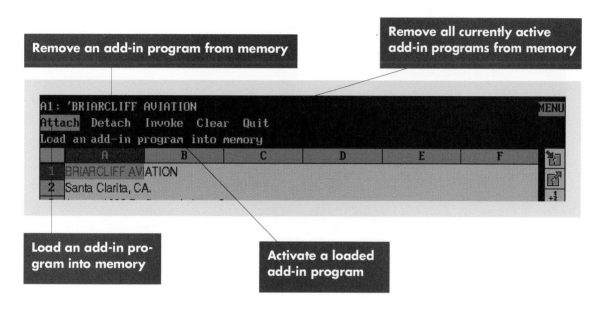

Remove an add-in program from memory

Remove all currently active add-in programs from memory

Load an add-in program into memory

Activate a loaded add-in program

3. Select Attach.

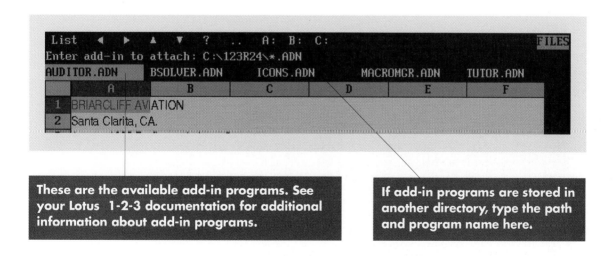

These are the available add-in programs. See your Lotus 1-2-3 documentation for additional information about add-in programs.

If add-in programs are stored in another directory, type the path and program name here.

4. Select BSOLVER.ADN.

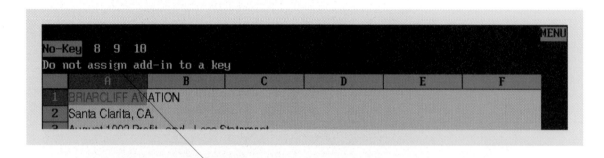

Designate a *hotkey* that you can press to invoke the add-in program at any time. As an example, if you select 8, your hotkey will be Alt-F8.

5. Select No-Key. You return to the Add-In menu.

6. Select Quit to return to the worksheet.

Solving a Backsolver Problem

Now that the Backsolver add-in program is attached, let's solve a simple problem.

1. Select /Add-In ➤ Invoke to display the Invoke menu.

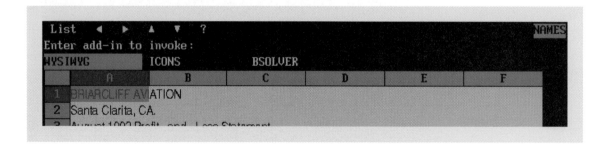

2. Select BSOLVER to activate the Backsolver add-in. The Backsolver menu appears.

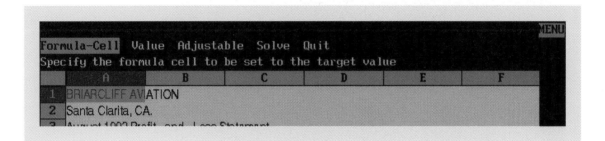

3. Select Formula-Cell and move the cell pointer to cell C12.

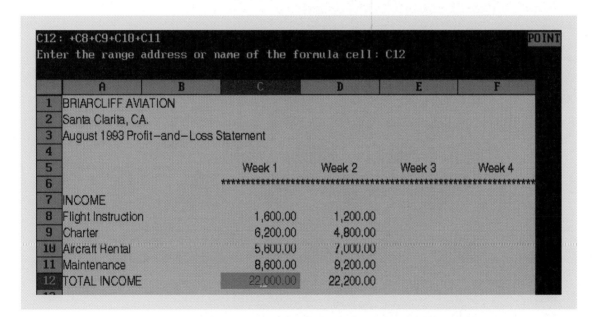

4. Press ↵ or click in the control panel to accept the formula in cell C12. The Backsolver menu appears again.

5. Select Value. You are asked to enter the hypothetical value for the formula cell.

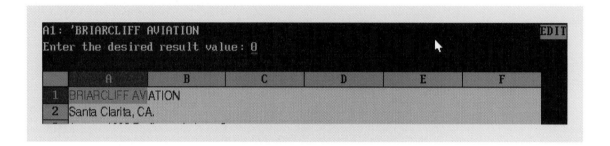

6. Type **24300** and press ↵. The Backsolver menu appears.

7. Select Adjustable. You are asked to specify those cells that you want adjusted to reflect the new formula value.

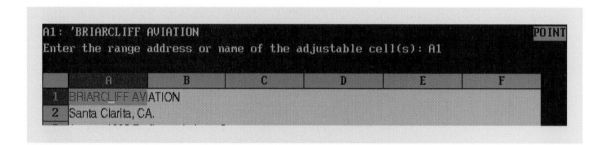

8. Move the cell pointer to cell C8 and press ↵ or click in the control panel. You return to the Backsolver menu.

9. Select Solve to solve the problem.

5		Week 1	Week 2	Week 3	Week 4
6		**			
7	INCOME				
8	Flight Instruction	3,900.00	1,200.00		
9	Charter	6,200.00	4,800.00		
10	Aircraft Rental	5,600.00	7,000.00		
11	Maintenance	8,600.00	9,200.00		
12	TOTAL INCOME	24,300.00	22,200.00		
13					
14	EXPENSES				
15	Wages	6,000.00	6,600.00		
16	Fuel/Oil/Parts	10,300.00	8,400.00		

Cell C12 now reflects the hypothetical total income.

Cell C8 indicates how much flight instruction income is needed to generate the hypothetical total income for Week 1.

10. Press Alt-F4 or select the Undo icon to restore the worksheet to its previous state.

11. Save the worksheet under its current name and quit 1-2-3.

PART FIVE

Transforming Worksheet Data into Graphs

After you create your worksheets, you'll probably want to use the information in some type of presentation. If you want more than numerical detail, you can transform the worksheet data into a graph. Graphs are great for representing relationships between numerical values visually.

- Creating and Viewing Bar Graphs

- Modifying and Enhancing Graphs

- Saving and Naming Graphs

- Printing Worksheet Graphs

5 MINUTES

Creating Bar Graphs 26

In this lesson you'll create a common type of graph, the bar graph. In this kind of graph, data is displayed as a series of vertical bars, each of which represents a numerical value.

Here, we'll copy data into columns E and F on the AUGPL1.WK1 worksheet and then create a bar graph for the INCOME items.

1. Retrieve the AUGPL1.WK1 file and move the cell pointer to cell C8.

2. Select the range C8..D21.

	Week 1	Week 2	Week 3	Week 4
5				
6	*********	**********	**********	**********
7 INCOME				
8 Flight Instruction	1,600.00	1,200.00		
9 Charter	6,200.00	4,800.00		
10 Aircraft Rental	5,600.00	7,000.00		
11 Maintenance	8,600.00	9,200.00		
12 TOTAL INCOME	22,000.00	22,200.00		
13				
14 EXPENSES				
15 Wages	6,000.00	6,600.00		
16 Fuel/Oil/Parts	10,300.00	8,400.00		
17 Rent	2,000.00	2,000.00		
18 Insurance	1,200.00	1,200.00		
19 TOTAL EXPENSES	19,500.00	18,200.00		
20				
21 TOTAL PROFIT/LOSS	$2,500.00	$4,000.00		

3. Select the Copy icon. You are asked where to copy the range.

4. Move the pointer to cell E8 and press ↵ or click in the control panel.

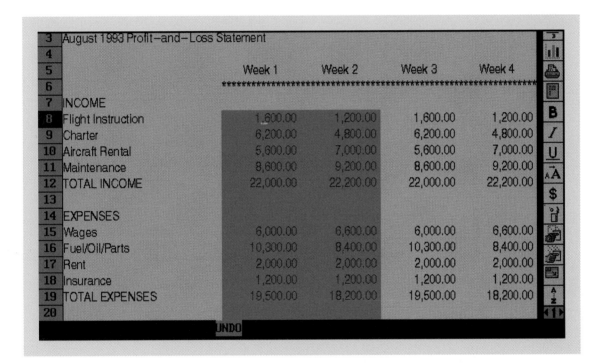

		Week 1	Week 2	Week 3	Week 4	
3	August 1993 Profit–and–Loss Statement					
4						
5		Week 1	Week 2	Week 3	Week 4	
6		**				
7	INCOME					
8	Flight Instruction	1,600.00	1,200.00	1,600.00	1,200.00	
9	Charter	6,200.00	4,800.00	6,200.00	4,800.00	
10	Aircraft Rental	5,600.00	7,000.00	5,600.00	7,000.00	
11	Maintenance	8,600.00	9,200.00	8,600.00	9,200.00	
12	TOTAL INCOME	22,000.00	22,200.00	22,000.00	22,200.00	
13						
14	EXPENSES					
15	Wages	6,000.00	6,600.00	6,000.00	6,600.00	
16	Fuel/Oil/Parts	10,300.00	8,400.00	10,300.00	8,400.00	
17	Rent	2,000.00	2,000.00	2,000.00	2,000.00	
18	Insurance	1,200.00	1,200.00	1,200.00	1,200.00	
19	TOTAL EXPENSES	19,500.00	18,200.00	19,500.00	18,200.00	
20						

UNDO

5. Press **Esc** or click on the right mouse button to remove the highlight from the range.

6. Select /Graph. The Graph menu and Graph Settings sheet are displayed.

Quick&Easy

```
C8: 1600                                                            MENU
Type  X  A  B  C  D  E  F  Reset  View  Save  Options  Name  Group  Quit
Line  Bar  XY  Stack-Bar  Pie  HLCO  Mixed  Features
                            ┌─Graph Settings─┐

 ┌─Type──────────┐    ┌─Ranges──────────┐    ┌─Orientation──────┐
 │ (*) Line      │    │ X: [···········]│    │ (*) Vertical     │
 │ ( ) XY        │    │ A: [···········]│    │ ( ) Horizontal   │
 │ ( ) Bar       │    │ B: [···········]│    └──────────────────┘
 │ ( ) Stacked bar│   │ C: [···········]│
 │ ( ) Pie       │    │ D: [···········]│    ┌─Zero line────────┐
 │ ( ) HLCO      │    │ E: [···········]│    │ [x] Y-axis       │
 │ ( ) Mixed     │    │ F: [···········]│    │ [x] X-axis       │
 └───────────────┘    └─────────────────┘    └──────────────────┘

 ┌─Frame─────────┐
 │ [x] Left      │     [x] Margins on        ┌─Grid lines───────┐
 │ [x] Right     │     [ ] Stack Data ranges │ [ ] Vertical     │
 │ [x] Top       │     [ ] 3-D bars          │ [ ] Horizontal   │
 │ [x] Bottom    │     [ ] Colors on         └──────────────────┘
 └───────────────┘

           ┌─────────────────────────────────────────┐
           │ Press F2 (EDIT) to edit settings        │
           └─────────────────────────────────────────┘
 2
```

7. Select Type.

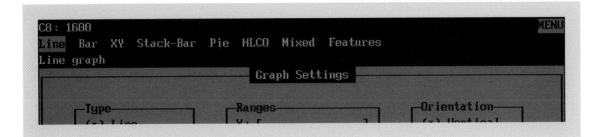

8. Select Bar.

> **● Note** Using the Graph Menu—Use *Type* to choose the type of graph you want. Use *X* to create labels along the X-axis (horizontal dimension) of a graph. Use *A* through *F* to specify up to six ranges of data to be graphed. *Reset* clears some or all of the current graph settings. *View* displays the graph on the screen. Use *Save* to save the graph as a graphics file with a .PIC extension, for use in a graphics program. Use *Options* to customize your graph. Use *Name* to create, modify, and delete named graphs. Use *Group* to specify several data ranges (in consecutive rows and columns) at one time.

Selecting the Range to Graph

You can choose up to six ranges of data to graph by choosing a letter *A* through *F.* You'll choose four ranges for this exercise.

1. Select A. You return to the worksheet to designate the first range of values for the bar graph.

2. Select the range that contains the INCOME data for Flight Instruction (C8..F8).

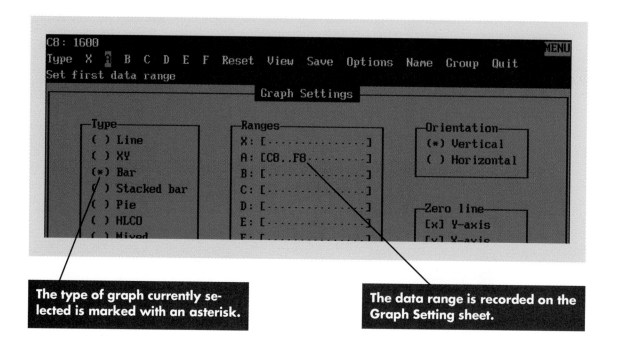

The type of graph currently selected is marked with an asterisk.

The data range is recorded on the Graph Setting sheet.

3. Select B, and then select the range C9..F9.

4. Select C, and then select the range C10..F10.

5. Select D, and then select the range C11..F11.

6. Select Quit to return to the worksheet.

Viewing Your Graph

You will want to view the results of your selection for accuracy and completeness before attempting to print the graph.

1. Select /Graph ➤ View, press **F10**, or select the Graph Display icon

on Palette 5 to display the graph.

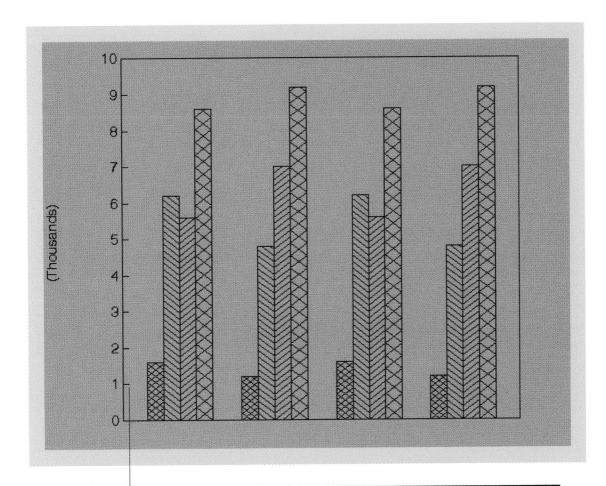

The vertical Y-axis values and tick marks are automatically created by 1-2-3.

2. Press any key or click the mouse. If you selected /Graph ➤ View, select Quick from the Graph menu to return to the worksheet. If you used **F10** or the Graph Display icon, you automatically return to the worksheet.

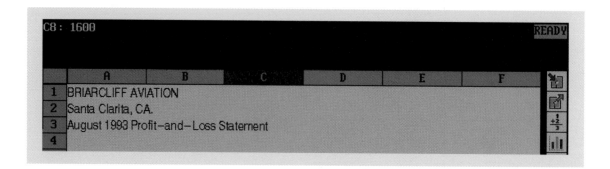

Keep this worksheet on the screen for the next lesson. (If you want
to take a break before you continue, be sure to save the worksheet as
usual, with the /File ➤ Save command.)

27

Enhancing Graphs

Now that you've created a graph from your worksheet data, you'll want to add some enhancements to increase its effectiveness. 1-2-3 enables you to add titles and labels, place horizontal and vertical grids, or change the scale used to present the data. In this lesson you'll make all these improvements to your AUGPL1.WK1 graph.

Adding Legends, Titles, and Labels

Legends, titles, and labels enable others to interpret the graphed data. A *legend* differentiates each data entry by applying different shadings and symbols. *Titles* provide an overall description of the graphed material. *Labels* are used to name each data entry.

Placing a Legend on a Graph

1. With the AUGPL1 graph displayed, select /Graph ➤ Options.

Places axis and graph titles on the graph

Creates a legend for all data ranges in the graph

Scales and formats numbers that appear along axes

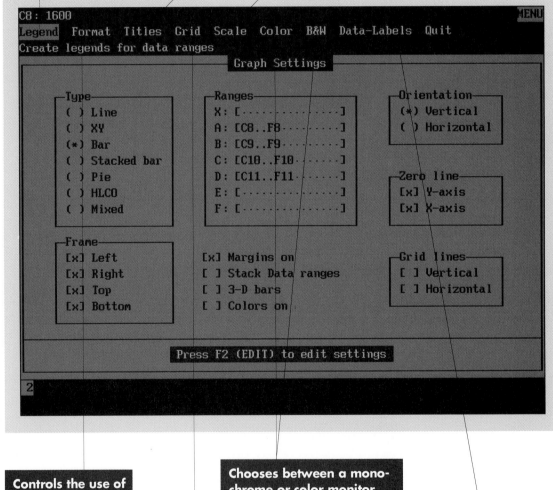

```
C8: 1600                                                        MENU
Legend  Format  Titles  Grid  Scale  Color  B&W  Data-Labels  Quit
Create legends for data ranges
                           Graph Settings
   ┌Type──────────┐   ┌Ranges────────────┐   ┌Orientation──────┐
   │ ( ) Line     │   X: [·············]     │ (*) Vertical    │
   │ ( ) XY       │   A: [C8..F8·······]     │ ( ) Horizontal  │
   │ (*) Bar      │   B: [C9..F9·······]     └─────────────────┘
   │ ( ) Stacked bar│ C: [C10..F10······]
   │ ( ) Pie      │   D: [C11..F11······]    ┌Zero line────────┐
   │ ( ) HLCO     │   E: [·············]     │ [x] Y-axis      │
   │ ( ) Mixed    │   F: [·············]     │ [x] X-axis      │
   └──────────────┘   └──────────────────┘   └─────────────────┘

   ┌Frame─────────┐
   │ [x] Left     │   [x] Margins on         ┌Grid lines───────┐
   │ [x] Right    │   [ ] Stack Data ranges  │ [ ] Vertical    │
   │ [x] Top      │   [ ] 3-D bars           │ [ ] Horizontal  │
   │ [x] Bottom   │   [ ] Colors on          └─────────────────┘
   └──────────────┘

              Press F2 (EDIT) to edit settings

 2
```

Controls the use of lines and symbols in XY graphs

Chooses between a monochrome or color monitor

Draws or clears grid lines

Specifies the contents of a cell (or range of cells) as labels for points or bars.

2. Select Legend. The Graph Legends & Titles sheet appears.

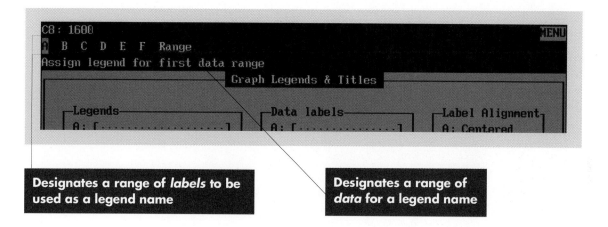

C8 : 1600   MENU
A B C D E F   Range
Assign legend for first data range
                    Graph Legends & Titles

┌Legends─────────────┐   ┌Data labels─────────┐   ┌Label Alignment┐
│ A: [............] │   │ A: [............] │   │ A: Centered
└────────────────────┘   └────────────────────┘   └───────────────┘

Designates a range of *labels* to be used as a legend name

Designates a range of *data* for a legend name

3. Select A and type **Flight Instruction**, the name of the first data range on the graph.

> **• Note** Assigning Legend Names—You can continue to designate legend names by selecting B, C, and D, and typing in the names of the remaining legends. Here, we'll demonstrate how to use the Range option to select a range of labels to use as legends.

171

Quick&Easy

```
C8: 1600                                                          EDIT
Enter legend for first data range: Flight Instruction_

                     ┌─────Graph Legends & Titles─────┐

┌Legends──────────┐  ┌Data labels──────┐  ┌Label Alignment┐
 A: [............]    A: [............]    A: Centered
 B: [............]    B: [............]    B: Centered
 C: [............]    C: [............]    C: Centered
 D: [............]    D: [............]    D: Centered
 E: [............]    E: [............]    E: Centered
 F: [............]    F: [............]    F: Centered

┌Titles───────────────────────────────┐  ┌Format──────────────┐
 First: [.............................]    A: Both    D: Both
 Second: [............................]    B: Both    E: Both
 X axis: [............................]    C: Both    F: Both
 Y axis: [............................]

            ┌─Press F2 (EDIT) to edit settings─┐

 2
```

4. Press ↵ or click in the control panel. You return to the
Graph Settings sheet.

5. Select Legend ➤ Range. You are asked to designate the legend range.

```
C8: 1600                                                      POINT
Enter legend range: C8
```

	A	B	C	D	E	F
1	BRIARCLIFF AVIATION					
2	Santa Clarita, CA.					

6. Highlight the range A8..A11.

		Week 1	Week 2	Week 3	Week 4
5		Week 1	Week 2	Week 3	Week 4
6		******	******	******	******
7	INCOME				
8	Flight Instruction	1,600.00	1,200.00	1,600.00	1,200.00
9	Charter	6,200.00	4,800.00	6,200.00	4,800.00
10	Aircraft Rental	5,600.00	7,000.00	5,600.00	7,000.00
11	Maintenance	8,600.00	9,200.00	8,600.00	9,200.00
12	TOTAL INCOME	22,000.00	22,200.00	22,000.00	22,200.00

> If you have typed in a legend and wish to use the Range option to designate other legends, you must include the first legend in the legend range.

7. Press ↵ and select Legend to display the Graph Legends & Titles sheet.

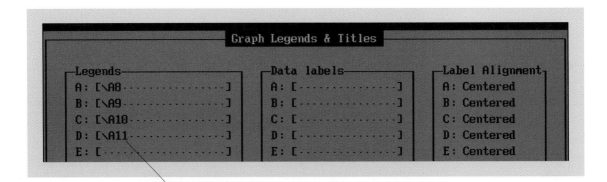

The cell addresses containing the labels to be
used as legends are displayed, instead of the
legend name.

8. Press **Esc** or click the right mouse button to return to the
Graph Settings sheet.

Placing a Title on a Graph

Now, let's further enhance the graph by creating two titles.

1. Select Titles.

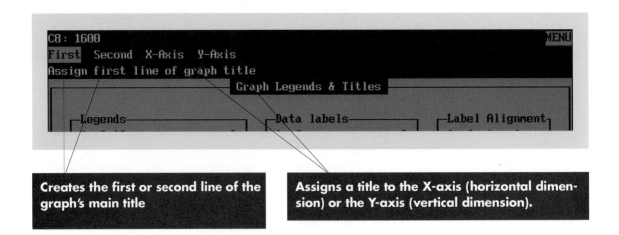

Creates the first or second line of the
graph's main title

Assigns a title to the X-axis (horizontal dimension) or the Y-axis (vertical dimension).

2. Select First and type **INCOME ITEMS**.

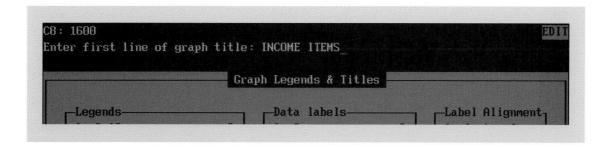

3. Press ↵. You return to the Graph Settings sheet.

4. Select Titles ➤ Second, type **August 1993** and press ↵.

5. Select Legend to view the Graph Legends & Titles sheet.

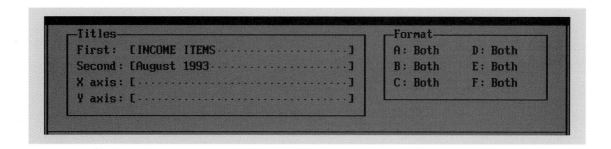

6. Press **Esc** twice or click the right mouse button twice to return to the Graph menu.

Placing a Label on a Graph

Now, let's label the X-axis of the graph with the Week-1 through Week-4 column labels.

1. Select X to place labels along the X-axis of the graph. You are asked to enter the X-axis range.

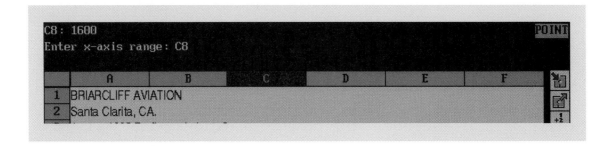

2. Highlight the range C5..F5.

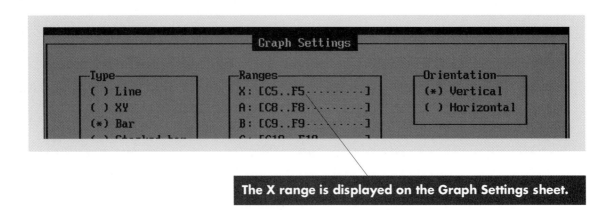

The X range is displayed on the Graph Settings sheet.

3. Press ↵ or click in the control panel.

Creating a Grid

A background grid on your graph can make it easier to interpret the graph's data. You can create three types of grids—horizontal, vertical, and a combination of both. Let's place a horizontal grid on the graph you're creating.

1. Select Options ➤ Grid.

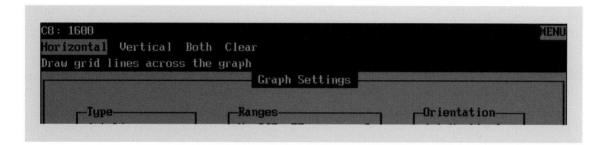

2. Select Horizontal.

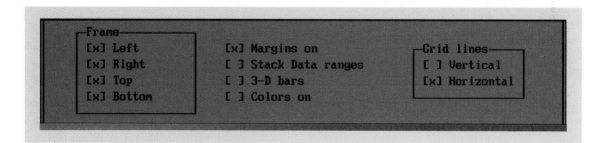

3. Select Quit to return to the Graph menu.

Changing Scale Lines

As you create a graph, 1-2-3 automatically establishes the X- and Y-axes according to the data selected for graphing. However, if you want to scale the graph yourself, you can do so. You can change the look of the scale indicators.

Let's modify the Y-axis on this graph by changing the scale and adding dollar signs to the scale indicators.

1. Select Options ➤ Scale to display the Graph Scale Settings sheet.

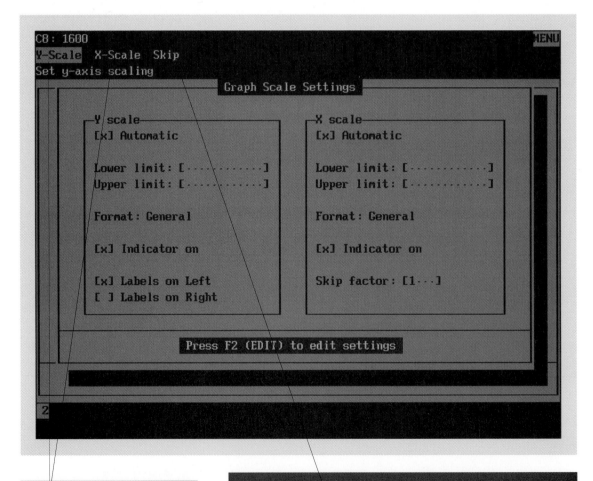

```
C8: 1600                                              MENU
Y-Scale  X-Scale  Skip
Set y-axis scaling
                     ┌─ Graph Scale Settings ─┐

      ┌─Y scale──────────────┐      ┌─X scale──────────────┐
      │ [x] Automatic        │      │ [x] Automatic        │
      │                      │      │                      │
      │ Lower limit: [·············]  │ Lower limit: [·············]  │
      │ Upper limit: [·············]  │ Upper limit: [·············]  │
      │                      │      │                      │
      │ Format: General      │      │ Format: General      │
      │                      │      │                      │
      │ [x] Indicator on     │      │ [x] Indicator on     │
      │                      │      │                      │
      │ [x] Labels on Left   │      │ Skip factor: [1···]  │
      │ [ ] Labels on Right  │      │                      │
      └──────────────────────┘      └──────────────────────┘

          ┌ Press F2 (EDIT) to edit settings ┐


      2
```

Sets the Y- or X-axis scale

Skips entries on the X-axis and displays only selected entries. (A skip value of 2 tells 1-2-3 to display only the first, third, fifth, and seventh entries, for example.)

2. Select Y-Scale.

Turns the scale indicator on or off. The scale indicator displays the scale units (hundreds, thousands, etc.)

Use in conjunction with the Manual option to specify the upper and lower scale limits

Makes the scaling process automatic

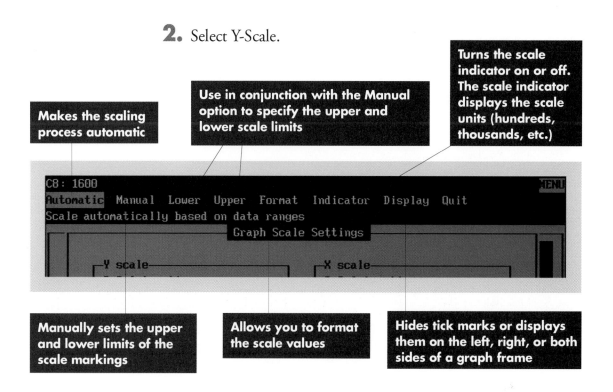

```
C8: 1600                                                        MENU
Automatic  Manual  Lower  Upper  Format  Indicator  Display  Quit
Scale automatically based on data ranges
                        Graph Scale Settings
      ┌Y scale─────────────────      ┌X scale──────────────
```

Manually sets the upper and lower limits of the scale markings

Allows you to format the scale values

Hides tick marks or displays them on the left, right, or both sides of a graph frame

3. Select Manual ➤ Upper. You are asked to enter the value for the upper limit.

4. Type **15000** and press ↵.

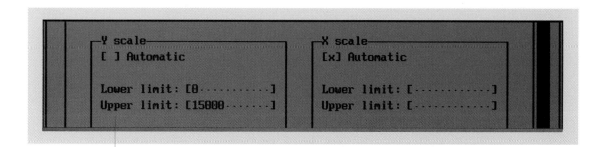

```
  ┌Y scale─────────────          ┌X scale─────────────
  [ ] Automatic                   [x] Automatic

  Lower limit: [0··········]      Lower limit: [···········]
  Upper limit: [15000·······]     Upper limit: [···········]
```

The Y-scale scaling display changes from Automatic to Manual and the upper limit changes to 15000.

5. Select Format ➤ Currency. You are asked to enter the number of decimal places.

6. Type **0** (zero) and press ↵ to prevent any decimal points from appearing in the scale indicators.

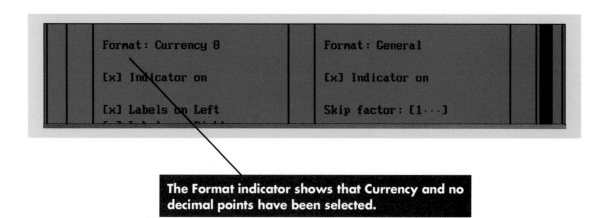

The Format indicator shows that Currency and no decimal points have been selected.

7. Select Quit twice, and then select View to see all the modifications you've made to your chart.

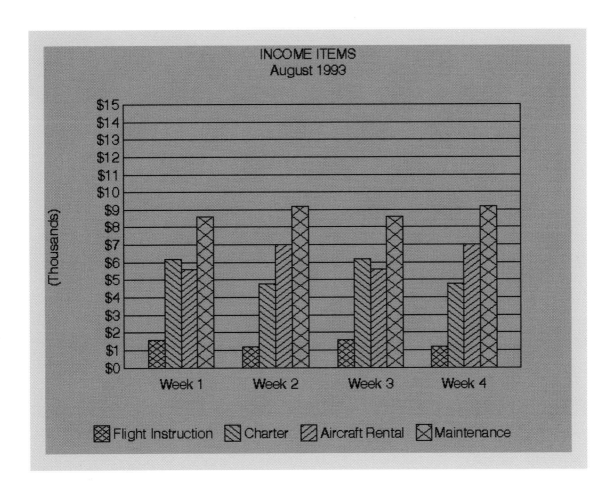

8. Press any key or click. Select Quit to return to the worksheet.

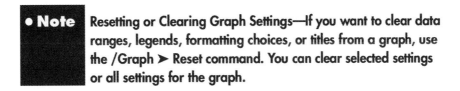

● Note Resetting or Clearing Graph Settings—If you want to clear data ranges, legends, formatting choices, or titles from a graph, use the /Graph ➤ Reset command. You can clear selected settings or all settings for the graph.

Keep this worksheet on the screen for the next lesson.

Saving and Naming Graphs 28

There are two methods for saving graphs. How you intend to use your graphs will determine how you save them.

If you will only be viewing your graph on-screen, simply save the worksheet as you have so far with the /File ➤ Save command. The graph settings will be saved with the worksheet.

If you will want to print your graph, you must save it with the /Graph ➤ Save command. This creates a graphic file with a .PIC extension, which can be used outside the 1-2-3 program. After you use /Graph ➤ Save, you must use the /File ➤ Save command in order to save the graph settings with the worksheet.

If you create more than one graph for a worksheet, you must name each graph before you save it, so 1-2-3 can differentiate among them. All the named graph settings will be saved when you use the /File ➤ Save command.

Let's name and save the bar graph for the AUGPL1.WK1 worksheet.

Naming Your Graph

1. With the AUGPL1.WK1 worksheet on the screen and the pointer in cell F10, select /Graph ➤ Name to display the Graph Settings sheet for the bar graph.

Assigns a name to a graph

Deletes all named graphs from a particular worksheet

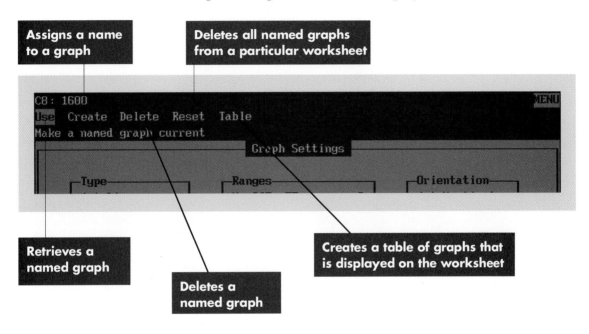

Retrieves a named graph

Deletes a named graph

Creates a table of graphs that is displayed on the worksheet

2. Select Create.

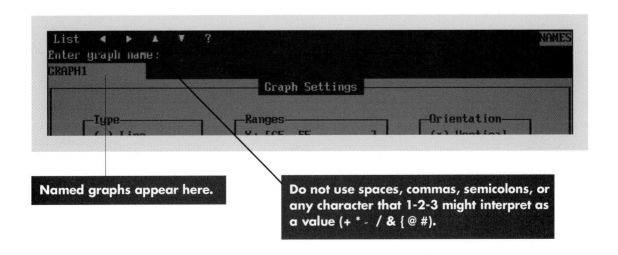

Named graphs appear here.

Do not use spaces, commas, semicolons, or any character that 1-2-3 might interpret as a value (+ * - / & { @ #).

3. Type **AUGUST1** as the graph name and press ↵. You return to the Graph Settings sheet.

4. Select Quit to return to the worksheet.

Saving Your Graph for Printing

Let's save a copy of the bar graph you just created (AUGUST1) for printing with the PrintGraph program.

1. With AUGPL1.WK1 displayed on your screen, select /Graph ➤ Name.

```
C8: 1600                                                     MENU
Use   Create  Delete  Reset  Table
Make a named graph current
                        ┌──────Graph Settings──────┐
  ┌─Type──────┐         ┌─Ranges──────┐       ┌─Orientation─┐
```

2. Select Use.

```
  List   ◄   ►   ▲   ▼   ?                              NAMES
Enter name of graph to make current:
AUGUST1          GRAPH1
                        ┌──────Graph Settings──────┐
  ┌─Type──────┐         ┌─Ranges──────┐       ┌─Orientation─┐
  │ ( ) Line             X: [C5..EE          ]   │ (•) Vertical
```

3. Select AUGUST1 to view the graph.

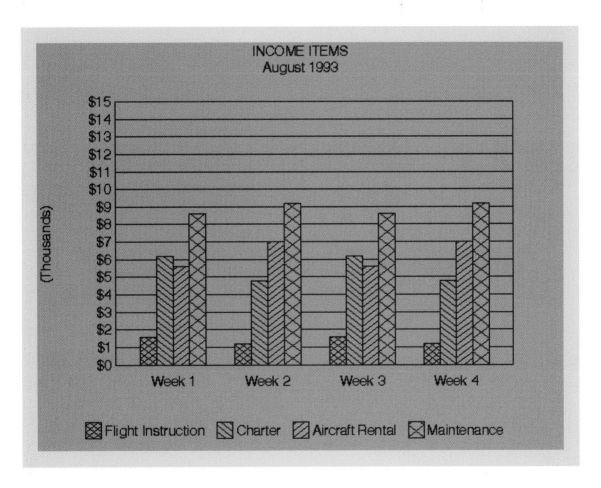

4. Press any key or click to return to the Graph menu. Select Save.

Quick&Easy

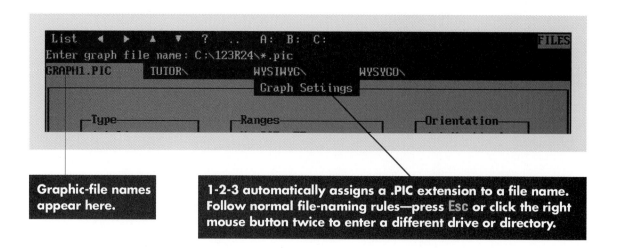

Graphic-file names appear here.

1-2-3 automatically assigns a .PIC extension to a file name. Follow normal file-naming rules—press Esc or click the right mouse button twice to enter a different drive or directory.

5. Type **AUGUST1** and press ↵ to name the graphic file and return to the Graph menu.

6. Select Quit to return to the worksheet.

Saving Graphs for Future Viewing

Use the /File ➤ Save command, or select the Save File icon to save all your graph settings with your worksheet.

1. Select /File ➤ Save and press ↵, or select the Save File icon.

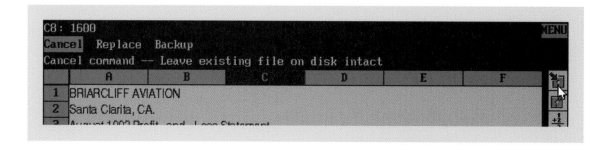

2. Select Replace to accept the AUGPL1.WK1 file name.

29

Enhancing Graphs

To print 1-2-3 graphs, you must use a separate program called PrintGraph. PrintGraph comes with your 1-2-3 program disks. You should have installed PrintGraph when you installed 1-2-3. If you did not, run the Install program and follow the instructions for installing PrintGraph.

Starting PrintGraph and Selecting PrintGraph Settings

Let's start PrintGraph to prepare for printing. Be sure your printer is on and ready to print.

1. If you are currently running 1-2-3, save your work and exit to the operating system or the Access System. If you exit to a DOS prompt, type **LOTUS** to start the Access System.

● Note Starting PrintGraph from DOS—You may start PrintGraph directly from a DOS prompt by typing PGRAPH.

2. Select PrintGraph. (If PrintGraph is not installed, you will receive an error message instructing you to install the program.)

Quick&Easy

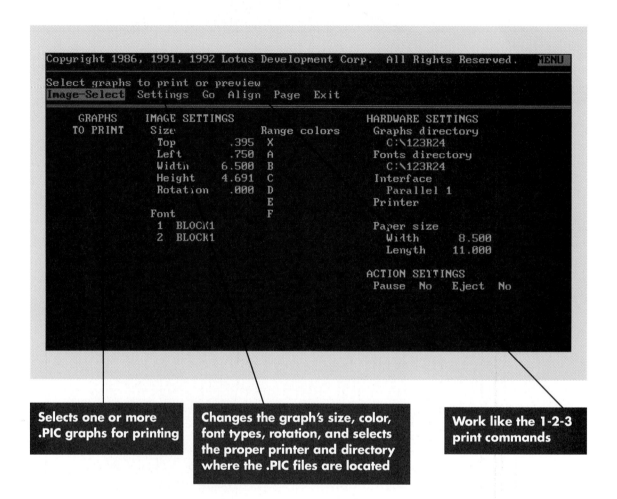

```
Copyright 1986, 1991, 1992 Lotus Development Corp.  All Rights Reserved.   MENU

Select graphs to print or preview
Image-Select  Settings  Go  Align  Page  Exit
─────────────────────────────────────────────────────────────────────────────
    GRAPHS      IMAGE SETTINGS                   HARDWARE SETTINGS
   TO PRINT      Size               Range colors    Graphs directory
                  Top        .395   X                 C:\123R24
                  Left       .750   A               Fonts directory
                  Width     6.500   B                 C:\123R24
                  Height    4.691   C               Interface
                  Rotation   .000   D                 Parallel 1
                                    E               Printer
                 Font               F
                  1  BLOCK1                         Paper size
                  2  BLOCK1                           Width      8.500
                                                      Length    11.000

                                                   ACTION SETTINGS
                                                    Pause  No   Eject  No
```

Selects one or more .PIC graphs for printing

Changes the graph's size, color, font types, rotation, and selects the proper printer and directory where the .PIC files are located

Work like the 1-2-3 print commands

3. Select Settings to set up the PrintGraph program. (You need only to do this procedure once, unless you want to modify the settings later.)

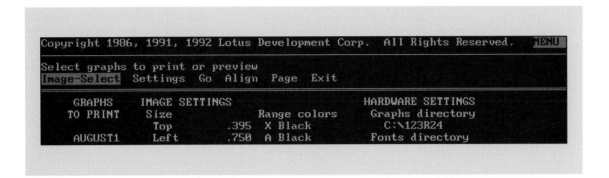

4. Select Hardware.

Selects the printer

Changes the paper size

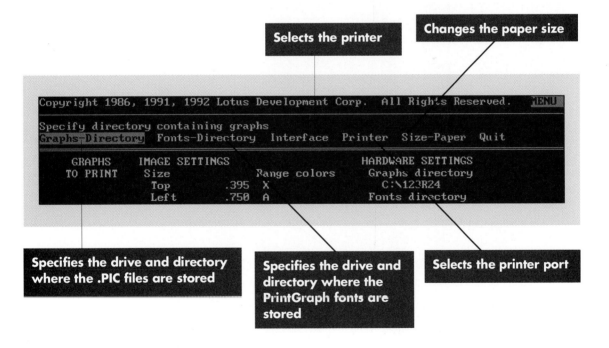

Specifies the drive and directory where the .PIC files are stored

Specifies the drive and directory where the PrintGraph fonts are stored

Selects the printer port

5. Select Graphs-Directory. The current directory is displayed. You can now type in another drive and directory if files are stored elsewhere.

6. Press ↵ to accept the 123R24 directory.

7. Select Fonts-Directory. You can now type in a new drive and directory where font files are stored.

8. Press ↵ to accept the current directory.

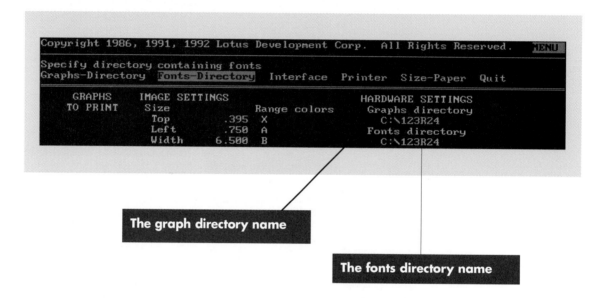

The graph directory name

The fonts directory name

9. Select Printer.

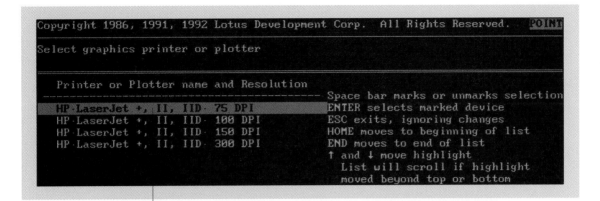

```
Copyright 1986, 1991, 1992 Lotus Development Corp.  All Rights Reserved.  POINT

Select graphics printer or plotter


   Printer or Plotter name and Resolution
  -------------------------------------------- Space bar marks or unmarks selection
   HP·LaserJet +, II, IID· 75 DPI          ENTER selects marked device
   HP·LaserJet +, II, IID· 100 DPI         ESC exits, ignoring changes
   HP·LaserJet +, II, IID· 150 DPI         HOME moves to beginning of list
   HP·LaserJet +, II, IID· 300 DPI         END moves to end of list
                                           ↑ and ↓ move highlight
                                             List will scroll if highlight
                                             moved beyond top or bottom
```

What printers are listed here depends on the printers selected during the installation of your 1-2-3 program. If the printers you see here cannot print graphs, you will have to run Install and install a suitable graphics printer.

10. Place the highlight on the printer and resolution desired and press ↵.

```
   GRAPHS    IMAGE SETTINGS                    HARDWARE SETTINGS
   TO PRINT  Size                 Range colors Graphs directory
             Top           .395   X Black        C:\123R24
             Left          .750   A Black      Fonts directory
             Width        6.500   B Black        C:\123R24
             Height       4.691   C Black      Interface
             Rotation      .000   D Black        Parallel 1
                                  E Black      Printer
             Font                 F Black        HP LJ 300 DPI
             1  BLOCK1                          Paper size
             2  BLOCK1                            Width       8.500
                                                  Length     11.000
```

The printer name

The range colors are entered as black because the HP LaserJet Series II does not support colors.

191

Quick Easy

11. Select Quit ➤ Save to save the print configuration settings. You return to the main menu.

Selecting Your Graph for Printing

Now that you have established your print settings, you're ready to print a copy of the AUGUST1.PIC file. Remember, you can print only graphs saved with the /Graph ➤ Save command, which stores the graph with a .PIC graphic file extension (see Lesson 28).

1. Select Image-Select.

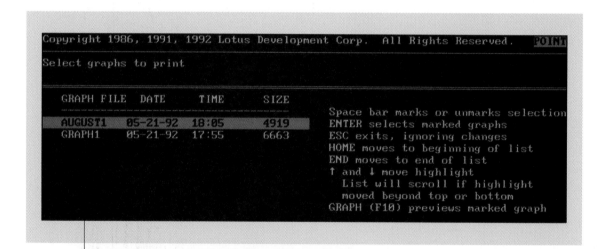

A list of all .PIC files is displayed. If the graph you want is not listed, you may be looking in the wrong directory.

● Note Viewing a Graph Before Printing—If you want to view the graph prior to printing, highlight the file name and press **F10** (GRAPH).

2. Move the highlight to AUGUST1 and press the spacebar to place a # next to the file name.

```
GRAPH FILE   DATE     TIME      SIZE
                                         Space bar marks or unmarks selection
#  AUGUST1   05-21-92  18:05     4919     ENTER selects marked graphs
   GRAPH1    05-21-92  17:55     6663     ESC exits, ignoring changes
```

When you want to print more than one file at a time, place a # next to each file name. To remove the #, highlight the file name and press the spacebar again.

3. Press ↵ to accept the file(s) for printing.

```
  GRAPHS     IMAGE SETTINGS                  HARDWARE SETTINGS
  TO PRINT   Size                 Range colors   Graphs directory
             Top        .395   X Black            C:\123R24
  AUGUST1    Left       .750   A Black         Fonts directory
             Width     6.500   B Black            C:\123R24
             Height    4.691   C Black         Interface
             Rotation   .000   D Black            Parallel 1
                               E Black         Printer
             Font              F Black            HP LJ 300 DPI
```

4. Select Align ➤ Go to print the graph. (If you are using a laser printer, select Page to move the paper through the printer. If you have a dot-matrix printer, select Page *after* the graph prints to move the paper through the printer.)

Your graph prints out. Keep the PrintGraph menu on your screen.

Customizing Your Graph's Printout

PrintGraph allows you to select different fonts and colors and to change the size of a graph.

1. Select Settings ➤ Image.

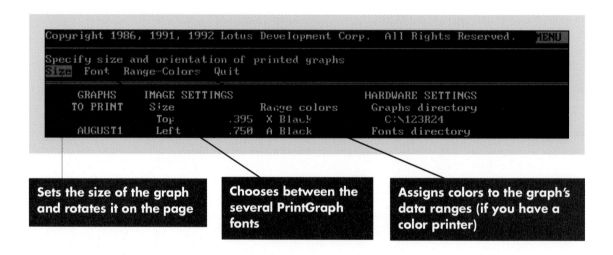

2. Select Size.

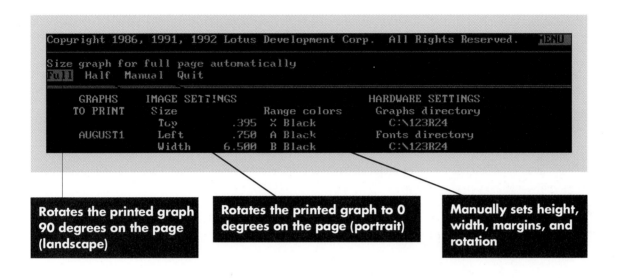

Copyright 1986, 1991, 1992 Lotus Development Corp. All Rights Reserved. MENU

Size graph for full page automatically
Full Half Manual Quit

GRAPHS   IMAGE SETTINGS   HARDWARE SETTINGS
TO PRINT   Size   Range colors   Graphs directory
             Top   .395   X Black   C:\123R24
AUGUST1   Left   .750   A Black   Fonts directory
             Width   6.500   B Black   C:\123R24

Rotates the printed graph 90 degrees on the page (landscape)

Rotates the printed graph to 0 degrees on the page (portrait)

Manually sets height, width, margins, and rotation

3. Select Full ➤ Quit to rotate the printed graph 90 degrees and return to the Image menu.

4. Select Font.

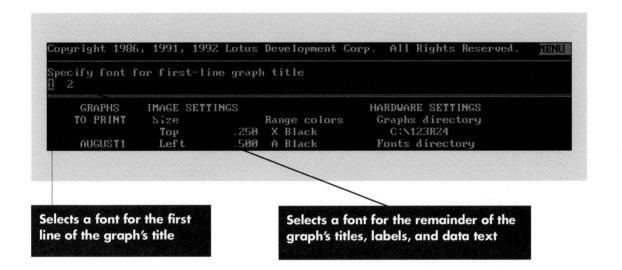

Copyright 1986, 1991, 1992 Lotus Development Corp. All Rights Reserved. MENU

Specify font for first-line graph title
1 2

GRAPHS   IMAGE SETTINGS   HARDWARE SETTINGS
TO PRINT   Size   Range colors   Graphs directory
             Top   .250   X Black   C:\123R24
AUGUST1   Left   .500   A Black   Fonts directory

Selects a font for the first line of the graph's title

Selects a font for the remainder of the graph's titles, labels, and data text

Quick&Easy

> **● Note** PrintGraph Fonts—Some PrintGraph fonts, such as Italic and
> Script, do not work well with dot-matrix printers. You may want
> to experiment with fonts to determine which ones work best on
> your printer.

5. Select 1 to display a list of fonts.

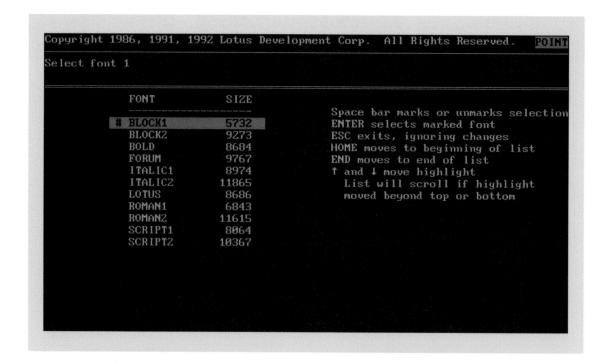

6. Highlight Roman 2, press the spacebar to select the font,
and press ↵ to change the first-line font to Roman2. 1-2-3
assumes you will want Font 1 and 2 to be the same, so Font
2 automatically changes to match Font 1. To select a different font for Font 2, repeat the procedure above for Font 2.

7. Select Quit twice to return to the PrintGraph menu.

8. Select Align ➤ Go ➤ Page to print the graph.

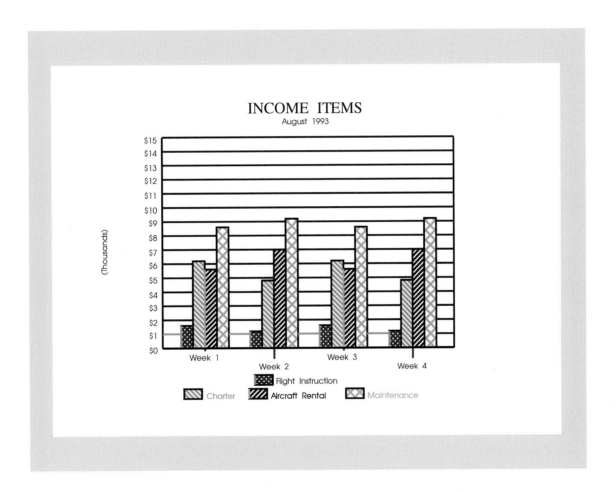

9. Select Exit ➤ Yes to return to the Access System.

10. Select Exit to return to DOS.

Where Do I Go from Here?

Now that you've finished with this book, you've learned what you need to know to get up and running with 1-2-3 in the shortest time possible. You know the basics, but 1-2-3 is a very powerful program with many other useful features you'll want to learn about eventually. For example, you may want to know how to make worksheet comments, such as brief descriptions of worksheets' contents or personal notes or reminders; or how to open worksheet windows, so you can view two different areas of the same worksheet; or how to protect data, to prevent all or a portion of the worksheet from being edited; or how to modify 1-2-3's default settings; or how to take advantage of 1-2-3's advanced printing options, such as making headers and footers, printing borders and cell formulas, and changing print size and margins; or how to share data with other programs; or how to work with macros.

If you'd like to stick with a beginner's approach, learning in short, easy lessons and trying things out step-by-step, then **ABC's of 1-2-3 Release 2.4 for DOS**, Chris Gilbert and Laurie Williams, SYBEX, 1992, is the right book for you. It covers the material in this book with a little more explanation, and then continues on and explains some of the more useful advanced features.

If you think you're ready for a how-to book that doubles as a reference and covers 1-2-3 in depth, try **Understanding 1-2-3 Release 2.3 & 2.4 for DOS**, Rebecca Bridges Altman, SYBEX, 1992. It's full of great examples and hands-on steps, and it explains everything from the most basic topics to the most advanced.

If you'd like a quick reference book to answer occasional questions, then you want **Lotus 1-2-3 Release 2.3 & 2.4 for DOS Instant Reference**, Judd Robbins, SYBEX, 1992.

INDEX

Note. Page numbers in Part One are purple.
Page numbers in Part Two are blue.
Page numbers in Part Three are green.
Page numbers in Part Four are orange.
Page numbers in Part Five are purple.

G

H